Get Over It!
How to Bounce Back
After Hitting Rock Bottom II

"Tragedy to Triumph"

Adair White-Johnson, Ph.D.

and

Contributing Authors

**Dr. Sondra Beall-Davis *Reva Dean *Naeema
Finley *Dr. LaToya N. Griffin *Jae Haeri*

**Leslie G. Howell *Tamiko Lowry-Pugh *Nicole
Morris *Tuesday S. White*

ADAIR WHITE JOHNSON
The Empowerment House & Johnson Tribe Publishing

Manufactured in the United States of America

Cataloging-in-Publication data for this book is available from the Library of Congress

ISBN-13:978-1-7337844-1-2

FIRST EDITION – March 2019

SECOND EDITION- February 2020

Creative Direction: Johnson Tribe Publishing, LLC

Book Cover Design: August Pride, LLC

Editing: White Standard Press

USA $19.95 Canada $24.95

Dedication

This book is dedicated to all of the courageous women who have hit rock bottom but found the strength to bounce back and

"Get Over It."

Contents

Introduction

Dr. Adair

I absolutely love writing and sharing the stories of courageous women who dared to find the strength to change their life circumstances. This book includes the testimonies of nine tenacious, diligent and influential women who have hit rock bottom but discovered their inner (strength) to find their way back up again.

Each story has been written from the heart of their experiences, and they share their journeys from "tragedy to triumph" to motivate, empower, and inspire you to move toward positive changes in your life.

As the Editor of this collaborative book, I wanted to begin with my own message of hope and faith for you. When I wrote this message, it was based on my own personal experiences and what I learned so that I can "trust the process." Enjoy!

Trust the Process

Very often, when I am on the speaking circuit and I meet many different people from all walks of life, I realize that they have no idea about the things I've done to prepare for that moment in time. They do not understand the culmination of my efforts to reach the point in my life where I am. They don't know the process and only see the end product.

1

That's what I want to write about today; "The process" and learning how to trust it to reach your end product.

Based upon my bio that's often printed or read before I speak and present, you can't tell from the bio that I was a child who grew up in Brooklyn in a tenement/building without heat or hot water. Life was really challenging.

I remember when we used to turn the stove on and close the dining room door just so we could stay warm. We lived with my grandmother, and we used to sleep on the floor in the dining room with a vast tapestry of Jesus on top of us and lots of winter coats thrown on top of us. I also remember that we had to boil water to take baths because we never had hot water. Times were just rough back then.

I also lived with a physical, emotional, psychologically abusive mother. You see, she was an alcoholic who died at the tender age of 37 when I was only 14 years old from cirrhosis of the liver. There was a lot of "stuff" that I had to endure while growing up but I learned as a child that this was just a part of the "process" that would allow me to become the end product.

I never felt special because I went through "stuff" in my childhood. I felt special because of the way I dealt with the stuff. The way I learned how to prepare for the process became essential for me, and I focused on what I did, how I did it and when I did it. This became the catalyst for the strengthening of my educational, intellectual and successful journey.

Many times in our lives, we are shrouded in fear, confusion, and doubt, and that stagnates our growth because we begin to believe that we cannot do the things that God has intended us to do. We don't trust and believe, and we fail to "trust the process." It's like we want to be in control of it all, but we don't have a plan of action. If we had that plan and learned how to "trust the process," it could make following our dreams a bit easier.

I want to share with you some nuggets of wisdom, 4 lessons that will help you to "trust the process" and make it a bit easier for you to achieve your dreams.

1. Do It Afraid:

I think that *Fear* is the number one emotion that holds us back from reaching our fullest potential, pursuing our passion and persevering in our purpose. When we are afraid, we often are paralyzed in our movement and do not allow ourselves to follow the path that was created just for us. We limit our possibilities and impede our success because we are afraid.

We have a fear of the unknown.

A fear of things known.

Fear of love.

Fear of failure.

Fear of success.

Fear of joy.

Fear of pain.

Fear of today and fear of tomorrow.

For some of us, we live a life in fear daily, and we do not allow ourselves to push through the struggle and become significant in our dreams.

It happens to the best of us.

And it can happen when we least expect it.

But it doesn't always have to be that way. If you create a plan of action, then it reduces that fear because you know that "the best is yet to come," and perhaps you will be willing to take more risks. This is all a part of the process, and you have to trust it!

You have to allow yourself to take chances.

Allow yourself to learn new things.

Allow yourself to do the same things but differently.

Allow yourself to trust yourself.

And allow yourself to "Do It Afraid."

2. Know your value and understand your worth.

Throughout my life, I don't think I ever really had a problem with my self-esteem or my self-confidence. In many instances, I may have been lucky because I know a lot of teens and adults really struggle to maintain healthy levels of self-esteem. I think I went through my teen years hoping and wishing that I had a bigger butt and bigger boobs, but I honestly don't believe that it really impacted how I viewed myself overall.

Somehow and someway, despite and in spite of the abusive childhood that I grew up in, my positive self-image was never destroyed. I know that there were some challenges to it, but because of my strong Faith and my belief that God created me the way I was supposed to be, I knew that I was valuable and worthy.

What I didn't know, however, was how to remind *others* of my value and teach them my worth. I think many people underestimate who they are and how much they mean to others and do not recognize their value or understand how worthy they truly are.

Or, they allow others to treat them "any ol' kind of way" because they believe that's what they deserve.

Wrong. You are only treated the way you allow yourself to be treated, and if you don't know your value and understand your worth, then you may underestimate what you deserve.

In trusting the process in your life, you must be willing to accept your greatness and know that you don't get to choose "nothingness." You don't get to decide that you are not worthy and allow yourself to be abused physically, emotionally, financially, spiritually, or verbally. You get to use the word "No!" as a complete sentence and stand upright beaming with pride knowing that you have already been bestowed with the jewels you need to be a King or Queen.

This is a part of the process! Knowing that despite where you come from, what you look like, what your parents do or don't do, you are worthy! Don't let anybody tell you are that you are not "good" enough, "smart" enough, "cute" enough, "dark" enough, "light" enough, "rich" enough, "relevant" enough, or anything other than "you are enough."

Growing up, I was always the "light-skinned, skinny with no shape girl," and so many folks around reminded me of that daily. My friends, my cousins, my family and sooooo many boys that I thought I really liked. Sometimes it hurt my feelings, but after a while, I realized that the stuff they were talking about, I really couldn't change.

I reminded myself that there had to be other things about me that were "good" enough and were worthy of praise, so I began to look for all the positive things in me to combat the negative things that others said about me. You know what I found?

My brain.

As a teenager, I discovered that I was really smart. I mean really smart. Beyond the "book" sense, I was actually quite wise because of my uncanny "gift" of analytical thinking; I was way beyond the thought process of many of my friends and family.

I realized that I often saw the world differently, interpreted it differently, and I saw people and situations differently. My brain became that organ that cultivated and encouraged me to look beyond the known and begin to explore the unknown.

A-ha!

This was when I knew that I was "enough." This was when I embraced that despite being light-skinned and skinny, I was still enough.

I was enough because I already had everything I needed to be that change agent in my life.

I was enough to follow my dreams and reach my destiny.

I had the power to stand in my truth, trust the process, and I knew that I was a child that God had created, and that was enough.

It was all that I needed to Know My Value and Understand my Worth.

You need to know this too. You see, you are already equipped and empowered you to become all that you are destined to be. A path has already been created a path JUST FOR YOU to travel along on this journey called "life."

And what's for you is already for you.

No one should be able to take that away from you because they didn't give it to you in the first place.

Don't give them power to take what is yours because you are worth more than that. You already have what you need to pursue your passion and persevere in the process!

You are enough to get the job done! And don't let nobody tell you anything else!

3. Get Out of Your Own Way!

Sometimes we are our biggest competitor, and we Get in Our Own Way.

We allow the triple threats of Fear, Confusion, and Doubt to stagnate our growth, and we forget to lean on our triple shields of Grace, Faith, and Mercy for the strength and guidance we need.

Sometimes it just feels more comfortable that way.

We often are afraid to venture outside of what is familiar to us because of the fear of the unknown and the fear of failure. So instead, we *never* embrace the concept of "being comfortable with being uncomfortable." I am sooooo guilty of this. I will actually talk myself out of trying something new by myself because I don't understand it, or I simply do not want to fail. What I have learned, however, is that I limit my possibilities when I do that. Simply put, I "Get in my Own Way."

To be successful, I've learned that we must take chances and allow ourselves to experiment, explore, and examine all opportunities. We just need to know it, and release the fear so we can *"Get Out of Our Own Way."*

The second thing that makes us stand in our own way is Confusion. When we position ourselves in front of our own success, it's often a consequence of us wallowing in confusion.

We are unsure of the next step, or we have too many thoughts at the same time, so we become confused. A mentor once taught me, "A confused mind does nothing," so when we are confused, we will paralyze our minds, and as a result, we do nothing. And the last time I checked, doing nothing does not increase our grades, work ethic and self-esteem.

All that it does is force us to *Get in Our Own Way.*

The third threat, *doubt,* emerge from the birth canals of fear and confusion. It is born when we are afraid and feel ill-equipped to travel on our unique paths, as though we are dogs chasing our own tails and just spinning around in circles. When we don't see forward movement, we begin to question if we made the right choice to become good students, exemplary athletes or extraordinary artists. We then start to question our skill sets, our abilities and even the gifts that God has given us. The birth of doubt in our lives tries to convince us that we are not worthy and we can't do it. We *Get in Our Own Way* because we give *doubt* a voice in our lives and often increase its volume a bit higher when we are afraid and confused.

So, what can we do?

Well, speaking from my own experience as well as the experiences of many others who have been successful professionally and personally, it begins with our mindsets.

First, you must remember that we own the power of change, so you have to learn how to use it. But you have to *allow ourselves to learn*. Give yourself permission to do things differently and approach challenges with flexible plans.

Second, I honestly believe that you have to check yourself to ensure that your personal "house is in order." I am talking about always knowing who you are, what you stand for, and what you believe in. So often, we get caught up in all of our materialistic things and how we can get more of it that we forget about who we really are, and we become disconnected from the core of our souls and the fabric of our spirits.

You will never be successful if you don't know, don't care, or don't like who you are at this moment.

The process begins with self, and sometimes it is a painful process, but it is still mandatory if you are going to learn how to *Get Out of Your Own Way*. This requires a relationship with honesty, truth, and transparency with yourself, and you have to be willing to discover who you so you can understand who you want to be.

You see, all of this is about a mindset. You have to change the way you think before you can change the way you behave. If you are successful in this mind shift, then you are steps closer to *Get Out of Your Own Way.* And if you do that, then you are steps closer to becoming that successful leader of your life.

You own the power of change. So change it.

Stop being stuck.

Get out of your own way.

Don't be your worst enemy.

Know yourself.

Trust and Believe in yourself.

If you can embrace the concept that you are in control of yourself, then you will know that you can morph into the person you dream of becoming.

You own yourself. No one else needs to validate who you are or what you are capable of doing because you own the power of you. With that power, you have the audacity to change, to make moves that point in the direction that your dreams are headed. But you have to want to change. You have to want it bad enough and be willing to sacrifice to ensure that you can make changes.

Don't allow others to control your existence and speak negativity into your life and stagnate your growth. That's not a part of the process. You own the power to allow you to live in the promised land that you envisioned for yourself, but you first have to learn how to Get Out of your own way.

4. Ask for Help!

You will also have to remember that it is okay to ask for help. Just because you ask for help doesn't mean that you are helpless. It doesn't mean that you are stupid. It doesn't mean that you are pathetic. It just means that you need help. You are not supposed to figure it out all alone. Many of us are surrounded by folks who want to help, but we don't allow them to. We put on our "Superwoman" or "Superman" capes and think that we can solve everything ourselves without help.

Wrong.

We all need somebody, and we all need help. You don't have to figure everything out by yourself. When we do this and don't ask for help, we keep doing things the same way each time and expect different results. Hmmmm...I think that's the definition of "crazy!"

Part of the process is allowing yourself to ask for help if you needed. You are not weak because you asked for help.

You should embrace that you don't have to do everything alone or figure it all out yourself.

You can accept help and still be strong.

You can accept help and still be an effective leader.

You can accept help and still be true to yourself.

You can accept help and still be independent.

And you can accept help and be thankful for the help.

It's okay. Just give yourself permission to ask for help.

Sometimes when we are trying to trust the process, we just need to ask for help to do it.

I cannot begin to tell you how many times folks will talk about the dreams they have for their lives, but when you ask them to share details, they are unable to do so. My mentor used to say, "A dream without a plan is just a wish." And there are a lot of people who sit around "wishing" every day and are unsure what their next step will be, so they become disillusioned. Sitting around and waiting for the dream to become a reality until they notice that someone else is living the dream that they thought about. Your dreams may have an expiration date on them if you don't make a plan to achieve them. Dreams don't come with a warranty or guarantee, and some of them have expiration dates. Begin to create and implement an action plan and trust the process to get there.

Follow your unique path and climb the steps that have been ordered just for you! It may get a little rough out there, and there are times when you feel:

Damaged, but know that you are not destroyed.

And you may feel bent, but you are not broken.

Your heart may feel discouraged, but that doesn't mean it's been defeated.

Your soul may be a bit tattered, but it's not torn.

And the trials and tribulations that you are experiencing today will be your truth and your triumph for tomorrow.

And even if you feel like a victim today, tomorrow is just a day away, and you will be victorious. You just have to trust the process.

So there you have it, four life lessons to help you along this journey to your dreams.

I know you have it in you. Don't let anyone tell you otherwise. Be mindful that everyone sitting in the front row is not clapping for you. Sometimes you have to look waaaaaay in the back of the room to find your greatest supporters. But they are there. Use them to motivate, inspire, and empower you to create those action plans to follow your dreams. Use what you have to get what you need. It's already inside of you. You got this. You only have to trust the process, and this will allow you to bounce back after hitting rock bottom so you can ***GET OVER IT!!!***

Dr. Sondra Beall-Davis

Servant of God, Dr. Sondra Beall-Davis, is the founder of "Klassic Training & Development"; a faith-based organization with the mission of making social change within learning communities. Her expertise is leadership and development with an emphasis on inclusion, diversity, and culturalization. She is a graduate of The Potter's House School of Ministry (PHSOM), has earned a Bachelor of Science degree from Dallas Baptist University (Dallas, Texas) in Management Information Systems (MIS), a Masters of Science in Business and HR (Human Relations) from Amberton University (Garland, Texas), and a doctoral (Ph.D.) of Applied Management and Decision Sciences from Walden University (Minneapolis, MN) specializing in Learning Management and Leadership Development.

For a just man falleth seven times, and riseth up again: but the wicked shall fall into mischief (Proverbs 24:16, KJV).

"We Fall Down"

Who Me: Angry Black Woman?

Over the years, I've found that some people perceived me as being too independent, verbal, and aggressive at times, especially when it comes to men and relationships. Perhaps I've inherited the reputation because I've found it almost impossible to find a reliable, trustworthy, or a responsible Black man to have as a suitable companion in my past.

I have cried and gotten angry about being alone. I had even felt alone when I was married, and when I became a single parent. Neither the man I married nor the ones I dated afterward were companions who could be trusted, responsible, or dependable. Each one left me infuriated with a broken heart that sometimes took years to heal; years that could never be recovered.

Perhaps my delegation of being the "Angry Black Woman" stems from the inability to forgive in the earlier years of my brokenness. As I matured over the years and learned more about God, my ability to forgive has become more comfortable. There is a passage in the King James Version of The Holy Bible that states:

"And the Lord said, if ye had faith as a grain of a mustard seed, ye might say unto this sycamine tree, be thou plucked up by the root, and be thou planted in the sea; and it should obey you." (Luke 17:6, KJV)

The reason this scripture is so important to me is that the sycamine tree is symbolic of how unforgiving people become entrenched in bitterness and hatred, ultimately dying inside. The sycamine tree was primarily used to build caskets in Jesus's time, growing more than 30 feet above the ground – symbolic of a direct relationship to death. It had an extensive and in-depth root system that grew into the depths of the water beneath the desert terrain. The roots grew so deep into the ground that uprooting the tree was almost impossible. Merely removing the stump of the tree wouldn't kill the roots that grew deep in the desert terrain. Each main root had to be dug out and removed from the source one root at a time. How the roots of the sycamine tree were removed to ensure the tree was dead is symbolic of harboring unforgiveness, deeply rooted in our hearts, bodies, and soul.

Through unforgiveness, we become deep-rooted trees that branch into tainted and bitter individuals, riddled with vindictive hatefulness from past hurtful experiences, rejection, and disappointments, dwelling in dry places like the sycamine tree. To become free from the entrapment of the deep-rooted pains of the past, each experience must be dug up and dealt with one person, one pain at a time. Continuing to house old wounds that bury animosity in our hearts against those who harm us promote the inability to build healthy relationships and truly love again (etc., husbands or wives, children, friends, even in the workplace).

The reality is that forgiveness is not for those who hurt us, but for those who want peace and the ability to move forward with their lives. Forgiveness removes the barriers that waste precious energy and time devoted to hurtful past experiences and allows you to become more focused on your true purpose and destiny as designed by God. I've asked God to heal my brokenness, my unforgiving heart, believing that if I only have the faith of a mustard seed, he would change me and free me from the imminent death of the soul created by hostilities. It's a slow process, yet each day I find myself forgiving those that hurt me one by one, removing the darkness of pain and rejection that dwelled so deeply rooted in me for so many years.

As for other Black Women who dwelled in dry and painful places as noted in the symbolism of the sycamine tree, "The Angry Black Woman" stereotype could be a manifestation that comes from becoming complacent with the disappointments of life and loveless relationships. Perhaps they secretly hide the fact that the pain and rejection run deep down, unaware of how this pain is irradiated in their faces when interacting with others. Perhaps they would rather stay in an abusive relationship rather than being alone.

I hypothesize that although many of our women encounter loveless relationships and harbor the lack of forgiving in their hearts, they are unwilling to move forward due to the fears of being alone. Perhaps they've given up on ever finding all the things that God warrants from our men? A man who is a true leader of the family, a powerful protector, and provider?

My perception is that many of our women are willing to settle by accepting men who have turned their backs on God's hierarchy, leaning towards the needs of the flesh. They've lowered their requirements and expectations to merely having a man to lay next to them -- any man regardless of his character and integrity. I think that those sisters who chose to settle and traveled the road of disenchantment with Black men and tainted relationships unintentionally or unconsciously promote "The Mad Black Woman" myths and characterizations.

As I reflect on my life, each of my encounters decreased all aspirations of ever having a fulfilling relationship. I'm not saying all Black men are irresponsible, lack integrity, deadbeat, uneducated, nor bad fathers; it's just that it seems Black women have more experiences with the absence of companionship and dependable fathers than most. My perception is that although outwardly angered faces and aggressive attitudes are frequently reflected in the faces of our Black women, it's often due to the ongoing persecutions encountered in daily life. I think that the best way to describe the faces of disenchantment is not that Black women are angry. Instead, they are heavy-hearted and tired of dealing with relationships riddled with surmountable pressures, ill-treatment, and lack of respect.

My thoughts are that we outwardly portray the negative images encompassed as anger and frustrations because we are tired of starving for love, irrefutable support, protection, and provisions from our men. Although I am not the voice for all Black women, I do feel that the perpetual "Angry Black Woman" stereotyping of our women doesn't take into consideration that our women are just tired of being the only parent and breadwinners of our families. Although easier said than done, to move forward, we as Black women must forgive those who hurt us and lean on God to fulfill our need for love, and sincere commitments in our marriages and relationships.

Dysfunction Junction: Turmoil at its Best!

The term "heavy-heartedness" truly addresses my own life. It not only refers to my troubles with men but my experience in general. As a child, the environment I grew up in was filled with crime, poverty, prostitution, and deceptive practices. As an adolescent and young adult, I never really realized that I was raised in an extremely dysfunctional environment; it didn't feel abnormal at the time. My mother was a good provider; she raised my two brothers and me by successfully shielding us from what could have been viewed as poverty and dysfunction.

In my earlier teenage years, I started to realize that some of the things she did to provide for us were not always ethically moral. For example, philandering behavior for material and financial gain. I'm very grateful to my mother for all that she did for us, but many of her decisions in life placed a wedge in our relationship. I didn't always agree with how she did things, but at the end of the day, I loved my Mama.

She was beautiful in her earlier years. Any room could easily be illuminated if she walked in, even if 100 women were occupying the same space. For her whole life, from youth up until her health started to fail in her 60's and 70's, I always heard my mother was drop-dead gorgeous. She was tall and fair-skinned with light brown eyes that complimented a million-dollar smile. When I was a little girl, I wanted so much to grow up to look like her, but the only thing I heard was, "you look just like your daddy"! It was not that my father was an unattractive man, I just wanted to look more like my mother because of her undeniable beauty.

Men went crazy over her; therefore, charisma and looks became survival tools. As I think back over the years, my incredible appetite to escape my environment could have manifested from watching my underemployed mother compromise her integrity to make ends meet. She'd been a seamstress at a local sewing manufacturer, a maid for some white folks, managed a teenage juke joint, and cleaned multiple laundromats. Yet, she never made more than what was considered minimum wage ($2 an hour) in the early 1970s on any of these jobs. If she weren't working on regular jobs, she'd be in hot pursuit of men for money.

As I think more about it, being abandoned at 9 years old by your mother and never knowing who your biological father was could promote multiple insecurities that lead to dysfunctional behaviors. After all, she had been passed around to live with family members who weren't really family, often stood in the shadows without loving arms, and felt she'd been on her own since age 12. She'd gotten pregnant before her 16th birthday, had to drop out of school, and was abandoned shortly after her pregnancy by my eldest brother's father.

My father entered the picture shortly after my eldest brother's father decided he would join the army and marry someone else. He'd married her knowing she would birth another man's baby and gave my eldest brother his last name. Although a hard-working, intelligent man, my father was also a high school dropout. According to my mother and other family members, I didn't think it was by choice but orchestrated through discrimination and barriers imposed by his own father. My father was medium built and handsome, with a deep dimple in his chin that complimented his smile. He was dark-skinned, much darker than several of his siblings. Throughout my childhood, my mother and several of my father's family members told me that my grandfather, a tall, slender, fair-skinned, grey-eyed man held biases toward the darker-skinned children. I was told that the darker-skinned children sometimes lacked preferential treatments made to the others, including displays of truly being loved.

One of my father's sisters told me that there was always friction between my dark-skinned father and my fair-skinned grandfather. It was to the degree that at one point, my father pulled out a gun during a heated argument because my grandfather tried to break his spirit by always talking down to him, being disrespectful, condescending, challenging his intelligence, and portraying him as a weak and useless individual.

Although my father didn't finish school, he became a self-made carpenter, an entrepreneur that could build immaculate homes from the ground up. He never became wealthy, but he always had a vibrant spirit. My father and mother divorced when I was in 2nd or 3rd grade in elementary school. The catalyst for the divorce came from my younger brother being conceived during one of my mother's rendezvouses and my father's infidelities during the marriage. They became toxic to one another. They always fought to the point of violence. This escalated to the point where my mother shot my father in the stomach when I was about 7 years old. The tit-for-tat infidelities within their relationship prompted their divorce.

The breakdown in our family structure contributed to significant dysfunctions that impacted my brothers and me. We were left without a father to lead and guide us and without a mother who really didn't know how to build a functional relationship with us. She didn't know what a functional relationship looked like.

Each of us dealt with the residual effects of having different fathers who had other children that existed, but not a real part of the lives of my brothers and me. My brothers gravitated toward street life, and I withdrew emotionally from my family. Although my brothers and I loved our mother, her dysfunctions became the link to our dysfunctions. As for me, her dysfunctionality created a bittersweet relationship.

Runaway Child: Chaos and Disappointments

One of the earliest accounts of my childhood was when I lived in a modest frame home that my mother purchased in the late 1960s. It was initially a boxcar that was framed into a two-bedroom house with a narrow front porch held to the roof by two wooden poles with pedestals. The front door was sealed with a mesh screen door that led to our small kitchen that had a back door with a small arched shaped window for viewing outside and three cement steps that led to our backyard coupled with shade trees.

My mother loved her backyard and would plant a garden every year, so she could have fresh vegetables and fruit that she would preserve for the winter. At the time, I thought we were rich because on the right side of our small kitchen entryway was a closet that had a built-in folding ironing board inside. You could open the door, let the ironing board down from its latches and raise it back into the closet to hide it from the rest of the tiny dining area. I'd never seen anything so luxurious in my life! It was simply beautiful! After all, before moving into our humble little home, we ironed our clothes on the foot of the bed or used an old standalone folding ironing board that had a torn cover and wobbly legs.

During those times, my mother gleamed with pride and happiness. It felt good to me too. Back then, it never occurred to me how a low income, underemployed, and uneducated single mom of three could afford the down payments nor the monthly mortgages that had to be paid for years to come. However, she made the payments and paid for the house over the agreed payment time.

The house is now a vacant lot. One of the neighbor's relatives, in the act of arson, burned down their home, and my mother's home was consumed in the process. My mother loved her little house. It broke her heart when it got burned. She always kept the inside and outside of it well-manicured, regardless of working around the clock and being underpaid by her employers.

She'd put as much energy in our house as she did get men to pay for it. As I was growing up, there were times I'd be in the car with her and heard her tell men, *"I'm not cheap, I got kids to feed and bills to pay; whatcha gonna do?"*

She'd been married several times over the years and loved to party at the local juke joints. The juke joints or nightclubs were the feeding grounds where most of her relationships with men occurred. I recall her coming from a club one night and saying that she'd met an extraordinarily tall and stout, dark-skinned man that worked cutting East Texas Pine trees for lumber. She laughed aloud saying he was kind and lots of fun. He lived in a rural community outside of our town. Within two weeks of that conversation, she moved him into our little house. This was when I realized that her behavior and motives were not always to find love, but a survival tool regardless of how she might jeopardize the safety of my brothers and me.

After about a year living in our home, it became evident that although there was no formal marriage, he was considered her husband by default under Texas law. *This is my wife…my old lady* or *this is my husband or my old man*, they'd say.

There had been others that moved in and stayed prolonged periods, but this one that I'll refer to as number three rubbed me wrong the first time I met him. At age 15, I'd run away from home due to fear of being raped by my 3rd common-law stepfather and my mother's dismissal of my telling her of his advances.

Since my mother wasn't trying to hear what I had to say, I turned to one of the administrators at my school. I told him that my common-law stepfather was always trying to get me alone with him, saying that he wanted me as his woman. I started crying, telling the administrator that I was terrified of being at home alone with this man. He asked me if I had somewhere to go and I said my father lived in Dallas, Texas and I could probably go stay with him.

The administrative assistant loaded me up in his car, took me to the local Greyhound bus station, handed me a sandwich, some chips, and $7.00. As I got out of his car, he politely told me to make sure I contacted my father, call him to let him know I was ok and to take care of myself.

That was the last time I'd spoken to him other than calling him to let him know I'd made it to my father's house. When I got to the Greyhound station in Dallas, a tall Black man approached me; he looked like he was in his thirties. He appeared so friendly and trustworthy, as he said... "*Hey, little girl, where you going,*"? I responded with I'm going to my dad's house; he lives in a community called South Oakcliff. I didn't know this would be one of my earliest encounters of angels appointed to put a hedge of protection around me. Lord, My God, I thank you!

The reality was that I was lost, I had no idea where my father lived, and no phone number to contact him. I was just a little girl in a strange place running away from what I felt would be my demise. The man told me to get in his car because he knew my dad and would take me to him. Without hesitation, I climbed in the car. During the ride, the man didn't murmur a word, he simply drove me straight to my father's house. As he parked in front of the renovated one-story frame home, he looked at me with a serious face, saying... "*Little girl, get out of this car, go to your father and "Never" get in the car with a stranger again!*" The man told me he could have done anything to me or taken me anywhere! He drove off as I started to walk down my father's red brick walkway, and I never saw him again. God had his angels over me then, and I didn't even know it.

After that, like a drifter, I stayed with my father and anyone who would let me sleep on the couch or the floor for about 6 months. This continued until one day, my older brother convinced me to come back to East Texas to stay with him so I could finish high school. Shortly after I moved in with my older brother, my mother threw out my common-law stepfather for incest. He'd impregnated one of his younger female relatives. Thinking that the coast was clear, I moved back in with her.

Although I'd moved back home, there was always conflict and chaos because my mother was constantly accusing me of the many men she paraded in and out of our home. One of the men she moved in had been incarcerated for murdering his wife and sleeping with her for a week after he'd killed her. Mama had the audacity of wanting us to call him daddy! The same man also held my mother and grandmother hostage at gunpoint in a laundry mat after my mother tried to break up with him. Thankfully he got carted off to jail shortly after the incident.

There was always chaos in my home. I would go to my grandmother's house and stay for days, stay with friends or family members, or isolate myself in my bedroom anytime a new boyfriend or potential stepfather came into the home. There was little peace of mind and stability during those days, so I pursued my East Texas high school sweetheart, as an option to marry.

Pandemonium: 16 and Pregnant

As if it wasn't enough pandemonium in my life already, at 16 years old, I got pregnant by my high school sweetheart, not once but twice within a few months. This was the straw that broke the camel's back, contributing to an already dysfunctional life. When I told my boyfriend, who later became my husband in 1975, he dumped me immediately declaring he wasn't ready to take care of a family.

The one person I thought I could depend on left me pregnant, alone, broken, afraid, and penniless. I had no one to confide in, nobody but Jesus, and I didn't really know Him at the time. What young girl wants to raise a baby without a father? I'd already seen that movie and how hard it was for my mother and other family members. I didn't want to be a single mother at 16 years old, desperate, vulnerable, and pushed to indulge in unethical practices just to survive. I merely wanted to wake up from the nightmare, finish school, leave town, and try to start over somewhere fresh.

There were no other boyfriends to step in, my father was pre-occupied with his new family, and my mother was too busy trying to replace the last husband. When I told her I was pregnant, she was livid and took me straight to an abortion clinic. Immediately after the abortion, I said to my then high school sweetheart that I had aborted the baby. He told me how sorry he was for leaving me and impregnated me again within weeks. For the second time, I went to an abortion clinic, only this time alone. I didn't know at the time that abortions were morally wrong, nor was I familiar with God's grace. At 16, terrified, ignorant, and depressed, I duplicated what I'd seen practiced by other members of my family. For many years I prayed that God would forgive me until one day I read 1 John 1:9;

> *"If we confess our sins, he is faithful and just and will forgive us our sins and purify us from all unrighteousness." (1 John 1:9, NIV)*

In the Bible, David and Paul were forgiven for committing murder, but they did not continue to commit murder after being forgiven. I asked for forgiveness and vowed never to take the life of another unborn child nor dishonor God ever again with the sin of abortion.

As a young adult, I learned that abortions were morally wrong and that any woman considering abortion no matter the reason must confess and understand it is forsaken (1 John 3:9, KJV and Romans 6:1-2, KJV). Abortion is never a solution to problems. If God is compassionate enough to forgive abortion, isn't He also merciful enough to help you avoid it? I've learned you can trust God with your life and with the life of your babies. I am transparent on my part of abortion, in hopes that others will seek God and turn to other alternatives.

Everyone that lives because their mothers decided to bear the pain of childbirth and take on the responsibilities of child-rearing should turn to their mothers and thank them for giving them life. Giving birth is a gift from God, a gift he will always provide for.

Heavenly Matrimony: To Hell and Back Again!

Looking back, I always knew in my heart that I loved my now ex-husband much more than he loved me. However, about a year and a half after the abortions, he did ask me to marry him when I told him I was leaving my mother's home again, even if I had to shack with someone – anyone! He'd told me he didn't want me shacking nor running away again but wanted me as his wife. His offer at the time seemed genuine, the answer to my prayers, even after being abandoned each time I got pregnant at 16; it was my escape from living within a toxic environment.

The man I married and lived with for 28 years became the vessel that freed me from encounters of verbal abuse and accusations from my mother. Marrying kept me from sexual advances and perverted ideas embedded in the heads of random husbands and boyfriends placed in a home that was supposed to be a safe place.

The first year of my marriage was one of the best years of my life. I felt truly adored and loved. I'd been through a lot, and he seemed to want to make reparations for all that had happened between us. After the first year, our marriage started to quickly deteriorate. There was minimal financial support, endless lies, multiple affairs, alcoholism, heavy marijuana usage, verbal abuse, and disrespect from my now ex-husband.

When friends or family asked about my marriage, I jokingly stated that my now ex-husband had several allergies:

1) He was allergic to faithfulness. Although we were married 28 years, I'd left the relationship feeling as though I'd dealt with at least 22 affairs over those 28 years. He'd always say, "You Can't Prove it!" as he walked away, smiling as tears trickled down my face.

2) He was allergic to truthfulness. He'd become a professional liar, so much that he started to lie about the lies he'd lied about; Lastly

3) He was allergic to work. He knew I was a provider and that I would work multiple jobs at a time to keep the family afloat. I'd travel to work on planes with tears in my eyes wanting to be home with my babies, knowing that rent, utilities, car notes, and college tuitions were due.

My life became a constant battle dealing with infidelities and loneliness. Each time I found out about an affair, I'd throw myself into my work or enrolled in a school to minimize the pain. I'd endure a lot, even being jailed because of one of his affairs that led to me being purposely rear-ended, ran off the road, and having a gun drawn on me by three women I didn't know. That day he'd left me vulnerable because of his infidelities, fighting for my life, the life of my eldest's son (at that time 9-month's old), my best girlfriend, and her baby boy.

A day that started out as a day of fun and shopping turned into a day that could have taken my life and others. God took over that day and saved me. Ultimately, I winded up in jail and charged with simple assault and put on probation for a year. This was the time I learned the names of the three women and what connection they had with my then-husband.

They were the sisters of the woman he was having an affair with. The sisters of the woman that was with him the day they ran me off the road and pulled a gun on me. Although I'd almost lost my life, I loved my husband, forgave him, and moved back to Dallas, Texas. Moving to Dallas provided me the opportunity to start over and wake up from the nightmare that seemed to steal any dreams I had at the time.

I believed in my marriage vows and wanted to make things work, although these were not the ambitions of my then-husband. I moved forward with my marriage as if I was an ostrich whose head stayed underground, ignoring the cheating, lying, and laziness. I'd decided that every time my then-husband did something negative, I'd do something positive (e.g., go to church and pray harder, work harder, go to school). I remember telling him that if he continued to cheat on me, someday I'd have a doctoral degree. He simply laughed, told me I was crazy and walked away. Going to school consistently and working endlessly to take care of my family when my ex-husband wouldn't work or took his money and gave it to other women became an escape mechanism.

Around year twenty of my marriage, I'd been blessed with a promising career at the executive level in corporate America earning a six-figure salary, earned a master's degree, and had given birth to three handsome sons. Most of my family and friends perceived me as having the American dream; they had no clue that my life was in shambles. I'd learned to mentally block out my pain and camouflage my reality from the eyes of the world. I'd become a master at hiding my hurt. During the last 2 years of my marriage, I'd gotten laid off my lucrative job, caught my husband in another affair, and was faced with declining health.

One morning after arriving at Dallas/Fort Worth Airport for a business trip to Houston, Texas, I'd blacked out during security check-in. I was taken to Baylor Hospital, where a specialist diagnosed me with a rare blood deficiency. As a chronic anemic, I was required to report to an oncology center 3 to 4 days a week 4 hours a day for blood and iron transfusions that lasted for almost 7 years.

This was the year I filed for divorce after finding out about the last affair I ever wanted to deal with concerning him. With a broken heart and failing health, once again, I greeted the world with fake smiles, fake conversations, a fake me. I needed to be strong for my sons, my babies; I needed to be "Super Woman." I struggled to keep what was left of our family together, although literally dying inside. My ex-husband left his family burdened and helpless.

I'd begged him multiple times to come home and work things out even after he admitted to having an extramarital affair. Serving divorce papers was a scare tactic to try and get him to stop the affair and come back home. My strategy failed miserably, he simply ignored and rejected me for months, and therefore I expedited the divorce process. I'd finally acknowledged the fact that he really didn't want the marriage to work, for if he did, he would have come back home. Expediting the divorce proceedings took me out of denial, I'd finally accepted the fact that my marriage was over.

I'm Just 12: Wearing Daddy's Shoes...

After my divorce, there were many days that I went into a mental shutdown, a zombie state, simply numb to everything around me. At 48 years old, I started to self-medicate by drinking heavily. I wanted to ease the pain but added another defect to my portfolio of crutches and "Holic's" (*workaholic, shopaholic, borderline alcoholic*).

I'd been told by my physicians that wine would help with building my blood levels, and it did. The only problem was that I didn't just drink one glass each night as advised by my doctors, I'd drink entire bottles of merlot wine each night until I became disoriented, then I'd pass out, including memory losses of what had happened when I was under the influence. The only thing that kept me going was the fact that I had three wonderful sons produced from my marriage. My eldest son was about to finish college, my middle son was preparing to enroll in college, and my youngest son, then 12 years old was at home with me.

The youngest had a front-row seat watching me drown in my pain. Yet, he never went a day without telling me, *"I love you, mama."* I felt so helpless because moral and financial support was non-existent for us. The abandonment of his father and the rejection encountered by our family members made my youngest feel he needed to somehow stop the pain. His father had walked away from both of us during the first 4 or 5 years of the divorce. He walked away from providing the love, guidance, discipline, and leadership that only a father can provide to a son. My interpretation of my ex-husband's rejection of my youngest son was that he had hurt me directly so many times over the years, the only method left to hurt me again was through my child, my baby.

Over the years, I'd learned how to teach my son's good work ethic, moral values, and how to pray to the Lord. But I couldn't teach them how to tie a necktie or stand up to use the bathroom. There were no tools instilled in me to show my baby to be a man, and no man was available to help me. Determined to stay afloat and maintain our household, I went into hustle mode and took my retirement savings and invested in a franchise at Farmers Insurance. My life became "Auto, Life, and Home" insurance sales, attempting to make ends meet with one-third of my previous salary, trying to pay college tuition for my two eldest children, mortgages, car notes, grocery bills, insurances, and utilities.

I no longer had the cushion of working in corporate to sustain my family. I'd cry constantly, had panic attacks that literally put me in bed for days, and felt as if mentally I'd simply crash and burn. My youngest son had seen too much, including paramedics setting bags over my face to control my breathing at least once a month. My baby became my caretaker when ambulances were not called; he would run and get a brown paper bag out of the pantry, cover my face to calm me down without guidance or instruction. Whenever I got ready for work and prepared him for school, he'd play my favorite song by Cameo called "Candy" just to see me smile and encourage me to dance around the room with him. As feelings of vulnerability, seclusion, and helplessness tiptoed into my life, my baby became my best friend and my protector at the age of 12. "*Just you and me Bud,*" I'd always tell him., *"Just you and me, Bud."* It was my way of reassuring him that no matter who left our lives or what happened in the future, I'd always be there for him. It was a pact made between us then and to this day – now and forever.

As if there wasn't enough darkness in our lives, things exacerbated; the one child that I'd always had a special connection with started to rebel against me. It was unbelievable. My eldest son turned on me. He became mean-spirited and extremely disrespectful, stating that I tore the family apart by getting the divorce. When I started dating other men after my divorce, he called me a "whoring harlot" and idolater that emasculated his father. He despised the fact that his younger brother was given extra attention from me because he had no one else at the time.

My eldest son, who was no longer living at home, dismissed the fact that his father had abandoned his 12-year-old little brother. Not only did his father abandon his brother, but he had abandoned him too! *My Lord, My God, what did I do?* How could I emasculate a man who refused to take on his responsibilities as a provider and protector, the leader of his family? My eldest now hated me and had no problem showing it. *My God, My Lord, Why?*

I asked God to heal our hearts, but it just got worse. Depressed and worried that neither daddy nor brothers would be around anymore, my baby went to the streets. He felt so rejected, he searched for his father's love thru street gangs and befriending drug dealers. At 15, he ran away and started a relationship with a woman twice his age.

After searching for my son for about 4 months via Wal-Mart's teenage runaway hotline, writing a letter to my local pastor and minister at the time, and the NAACP, I felt my son was gone forever. I'd looked for his body in a creek bed behind my house, drove to East Texas to see if any family members had heard from him, kneeling at my aunt and brother's gravesite asking God to protect and guide him. I was so tired and so sad.

One rainy day, I went to my ex-husband begging him to help me find our baby, he pushed me away and told me to get out of his face. Little did I know he was helping our baby stay in the streets. Instead of telling him to go home to a safe, stable environment and finish school, he dismissed his role as a father. Out of vindictiveness, my ex-husband hated me more than he loved our son and helped lead our baby to the streets. He rejected his son by watching him destroy his life, dismissing his role as a father. I remember sitting on the side of my bed one Sunday morning with a 24 pack of "BC Powders" on my bed stand. I was planning to put each powder in a glass filled with water when suddenly, the phone rang. It was my younger sister saying, *"Sana'jean, come to go to church with me."*

For some reason, I put away the "BC Powders" and prepared to go to church. As I arrived at a church I'd never been to before, nor did I know the minister, my name was called. The minister looked directly at me and said, *"Will you come"? "Sondra, Will You Come"? Your son will be home in two weeks; God heard you"!*

I hadn't given a testimony nor shared my story with him, he just called me with no knowledge of who I was; another intervention from God. Within two weeks, my son was picked up by police officers and taken to jail with his *pedophile* of a mistress. My son told me she was bringing him home, he'd decided he no longer wanted to live the life she offered and wanted to join the army. He joined the military and led a large aviation troop at the age of 17.

There was a lot of turbulence and instabilities in between and after these events, too much to include in this article (*a failed 10-year common-law marriage after my legal 28-year first marriage, disappointing dating attempts, new jobs and layoffs, and the loss of a $300,000 home in an affluent neighborhood*). My family members rejected me and wrote me off as mentally unstable as I roamed from relative to a relative like a homeless gypsy for more than a year and a half.

I was battling deep depression again. I'd been through on-going traumatizing events, then God called me, he put angels in place to lead me to complete a doctoral degree, two years of theology school, and now launching my own consulting company throughout each battle.

As a licensed minister, I have been called to serve and to help lead God's sheep. I've learned what's essential and what's not now. I've now learned God's hierarchy, boldly put on my armor and speak his word:

> *"Put on the whole armor of God, that ye may be able to stand against the wiles of the devil"* (Eph 6:10-18, KJV).

The Hierarchy: When God Calls...

I've lost a lot and endured indescribable pains over the years yet have faith that God will restore and deliver me as promised. As declared by Job:

> *"Though he slays me, yet will I trust in him: but I will maintain mine own ways before him."*
>
> *(Job 13:15, KJV).*

I, too have faith in God. Although I still have many battles ahead of me, I am grateful for the ones God has allowed me to triumph over. My journey has made me a believer in angels and miracles. It was a miracle that I graduated with a Ph.D. because there was spiritual warfare going on throughout the process – a battle I could not win on my own. God sent an angel, a stranger that co-signed for my last two years of tuition because I didn't have the money to stay in school. It was an angel that walked up behind me one day at church as I had tears in my eyes and told me God said I was ready and paid my tuition and enrolled me into theology school – unemployed and broke at the time. Although a broken educational system and predatory lenders left me battling more than $250,000 in student loan debt, I still believe that God will provide a miracle to erase all of it:

"And the LORD shall make thee the head, not the tail; and thou shalt be above only, and thou shalt not be beneath; if that thou hearken unto the commandments of the LORD thy God, which I command thee this day, to observe and to do them."

(Deut 28:13, KJV).

I believe and have faith in God's word; therefore, I cast my worries unto Him to provide, guide, and protect me:

"Cast thy burden upon the LORD, and he shall sustain thee: he shall never suffer the righteous to be moved. "

(Psalm 55:22, KJV).

I have no clue as to what is in store for me moving forward in my journey, but what I do know as written in a song by Sinach, *God is a Waymaker*:

"Waymaker, Miracle worker, Promise Keeper, Light in the darkness; My God, that is who you are" (Sinach, 2016).

God's word promises that my latter days will be greater than my former days, and I have faith in God's word:

"Though thy beginning was small, yet thy latter end should greatly increase" (Job 8:7, KJV).

My testimony is humbleness, trusting in God, and holding onto him through faith to gain strength and perseverance. Everything that has occurred in my life has helped me to understand the importance of life and how vulnerable we are without God guiding us. I've learned the hierarchy of putting God first by spending time with him to build a relationship, followed by family, then work to provide for the family. I don't have to be "liked nor followed" by others on Facebook, Instagram, or Twitter. I just need to obey God's word by scheduling time with Him. God's hierarchy does not include idolizing material things (money, big houses, fancy cars, bling jewelry, designer clothes, etc.) and it doesn't involve abusing power and influence if you've been blessed to have authority over others.

My testimony is to help those who have endured dysfunctional family ties beyond their control. It is for those who have suffered from divorce and experienced how it deteriorates family structures. I've suffered from abusive relationships that made me feel that I would never find real love; knowing now that God will supply everything I need - real love:

But my God shall supply all your need according to his riches in glory by Christ Jesus

(Phil, 4:9, KJV).

My testimony is for the women who had abortions that led them to deep depression as they were ignorant of the fact that it is "Not" of God. My testimony is one of broken spirits developed from living in toxic environments where domestic violence flourished. This testimony is of how loneliness, rejection, and abandonment can lead to suicidal tendencies and how using alcohol to self-medicate is a crutch that can lead to addiction.

Whether you believe in God and truly have a relationship with Him, or even if you are just a religious person or non-believer, to get through your journey, your storm, and survive the darkest days I share my walk with you:

a) Hold on to that rope of life, your hope and dreams that have become a single unraveling thread in life, and never let it go; it will only break if you let go because then you've given up.

b) No matter how badly someone treats you, forgive them and keep it moving, kill all the roots one by one that created the sycamine tree inside you - it's the only way you can move forward in life.

c) Detach yourself from those who display characteristics of jealousy, lack persistence in their pursuits; always put things off till tomorrow, never finishing anything – hardcore procrastinators; those that focus more on gossiping and being vindictive versus being supportive; those that have counterproductive work behaviors; simply put... non-eagles, but scavenging birds of prey.

My testimony is to profess that fear is a tool of Satan and not God. Repent and believe in the Grace of God. He can and will replenish the soul through restoration and deliverance. I thank God and the covering of the blood of the Lamb for all that I've been blessed to accomplish. *Hallelujah!*

Today, I am Dr. Sondra Beall-Davis or Lady Beall-Davis, a Sister in Ministry, a Woman of the Cloth -- God's servant! There is a hierarchy with God, and sometimes we must learn the hard way. When God calls you, you can run, but you can't hide. I'm so honored that He called me, favors me, and continually blesses me. There is no doubt in my mind that He will fully restore and deliver me!

Reference

Joseph, S. (2016). Waymaker [Recorded by Sinach Joseph].
Loveworld, SLIC. Retrieved from http://sinach.org

Good. Bad. Ugly.
Truth.
If it's yours,
Stand in it.

~Dr. Adair

Reva Dean

Author, Playwright, and Certified Relationship Coach, Reva Dean, resides in Nassau, Bahamas with her 18-year-old son, Rasheed J Francis. She is the founder of a non-profit organization, *Let's Give With Love* which empowers young people to believe in themselves and provides charitable donations to those in need. Also, as the CEO of *Beyond The Ordinary Enterprises,* she provides services for weddings and other occasions. In her spare time, she loves to sing, shop and spend time with her son.

"If it had not been for the Lord who was on my side, where would I be?"

~Psalms 124

"Walking in Faith"

The purpose of this chapter is to share my story about the trials and tribulations in my life that taught me how to be the strong woman I am today.

Throughout my life, I have often been a victim, but I learned how to be victorious. I want to share with you exactly how I did this:

Have you ever heard the phrase *"The struggle is real?"*

Well, I will tell you that these are some of the most real words I've ever heard. I've felt these words, lived these words, and survived these words. In fact, these are the words that would shape my faith, test my courage, and ignite my triumph.

The year 2009 started off great. I was super excited about the many possibilities this year

could have in store for me. I had recently gotten a huge promotion, bought a fancy new car, furnished my bedroom, and the world looked and felt amazing.

I was happy. At least, I suppose, that's what it felt like. Up to this point, to me, happiness was a strange feeling. So, I wasn't sure if this feeling was authentic, or just a mask of what I thought happiness should be.

I grew up in an unstable environment.

14 people were living in a small, rundown two-bedroom apartment in inner-city Nassau. The place we called Paradise was no Paradise for me. My mother was a single parent of three, and my father was MIA (missing in action).

My mother was there but only in the capacity that she could. She would work long hours at the hotel, and I'd hardly get to see her.

Growing up without a father was extremely rough for me. I couldn't understand the reason for him not being there.

In the place I called home, nothing was really expected of me but to *exist*, and that's what I did. I *existed*. There was no structure, no discipline, and the words "I love you" were never spoken. I never understood why.

Eventually, the feeling of not being good enough harbored within me. It led to a lack of confidence, self-respect, and low self-esteem. This all made me a target of bullying and peer pressure. The bullying was so horrible that I was afraid to go to school or would sometimes walk the long way home just to avoid being picked on.

This made me feel powerless and defeated. Yet, I still somehow held on to who I knew I could be. I knew that deep down inside, there had to be a plan for my life. So, I made up my mind to try and figure out what it was.

I remember many days going to school without lunch and abruptly running out of 1 and 2 periods to throw up nothing but my saliva. I would then painfully walk back to my seat, fearing how I would make it through the rest of the day.

By the time I was 12 years old, I had decided to get a job. I started working in the local straw market in the heart of Nassau selling t-shirts and souvenirs to the tourists to make money to survive. On the inside, I would have loved instead to be playing with a beautiful pink and white dream dollhouse with a girl and boy doll to match. Those were considered luxuries to me. I would only cry myself to sleep, knowing I would never have any of those things nor a chance at a normal childhood.

At home, sometimes I would lock myself in the bathroom and cry. I felt so alone, abandoned, and out of place. As the months stretched on, I prayed for my parents to be there and to remember me. I couldn't help but think maybe they didn't want me.

I often thought and asked myself, *"Maybe it's my fault. Why is this happening to me?"*

I had so many mixed emotions, and those emotions began to grow within me. I just needed a breath of fresh air, but instead, things got worse for me.

My mother had to completely move out of the house after an argument went south with her, my aunt and, my grandfather about closet space.

Now I was left to raise myself. Fear flooded my heart as I braced myself to struggle alone.

As a child of absent parents in the household, the other children there would get their way. They were awful to me. My complaints to the adults in the home often fell on deaf ears. The other children would eventually destroy my school books and uniform. You name it, they destroyed it. It got to the point where the school had to provide a uniform for me that a student left behind when she graduated. I was grateful and embarrassed at the same time. If the other kids at school found out, the bullying would become torturous.

I remember writing my first poem around that time my mom left. When I read it out loud, I got a standing ovation. I was happy, but then again, maybe I wasn't. The unfamiliar happiness faded when I realized that I couldn't take the poem home because there was no one there to say, "I'm proud of you," or any other words that would encourage me to keep writing.

A few years later, my mom came back for me. I felt a lot better, but the feeling of being incomplete still lingered. I wanted to find my father. I had questions that I needed to be answered, and I needed them answered now. I was angry.

My sister and I went looking for my father. When I saw him, touched him, and spoke to him, it took everything in me not to cry. My father seemed so cool, calm, and collected. I fell in love instantly. I had forgiven him unknowingly.

When I became an adult, I had a son. To no surprise, I became a single mother as well. The father of my son preyed on my lack of confidence and low self-esteem, leaving me broken.

I remember when my son was only a few weeks old, and his father brought some supplies for him. He started touching me inappropriately and tried to force himself on me. I demanded that he stopped and told him that I am wasn't going to allow him to belittle me. I was not going to have sex with him for him to provide for our child. He then decided if I weren't going to sleep with him, he would not take care of our son.

I realized at this point what I had to do. I had my son's father placed on official child support and he had to pay whenever it was convenient for him

Yet, even when he didn't show up, God still made a way.

God can put our pieces back together again when we fall short of ourselves.

My son is now 18 years old. He loves to dance and one day wishes to be an influential soccer player.

With the help of The Lord, it does not matter who we are, we can redeem ourselves and rise above the odds.

I can explain this more as you read on.

Let's go back to 2009.

One morning, I came to work very early. I worked at a beautiful office on Paradise Island where I sold condos. About an hour and a half into my shift, I got a call from my Supervisor asking me to leave my post immediately and report to the office.

I knew the economy was low, and there was a massive redundancy a few months earlier from another hotel. However, my Boss had made it perfectly clear that we were a small staff and that my position was safe in the company. After all, it was a wealthy company.

So, I was confident on my route to the office. When I entered the office, my supervisor asked me to have a seat. I sat in the chair closest to the glass doors that reflected the images of outside. When she looked me in the eyes, I instantaneously knew something was wrong. With tears streaming down her face, she began to give me the speech.

The speech. You know, the one that goes,

"Well, the economy is low, and the occupancy has placed us in a touch position. It's unfortunate for us that this is happening, and you were a great asset. But we have to let you go."

My son was nine years old at the time. I lived at home with my mother and had hefty bank loans. These were not the words a single mother like me wanted to hear. How was I going to explain to my mother that her biggest source of help was out of a job? What was I to say to my son?

I felt like such a disappointment.

The day that started off, like any other day, turned into a nightmare. I had to use all the willpower in me not to scream. I shook and trembled, realizing that the worst part of it all was yet to come.

I had no one to rely on.

My family had their own struggles. I didn't have many friends. You see, once the money stopped, so did the friendship.

I had no one rely on. No one, but God.

I left the office devastated as I watch my whole life go down in shambles.

Questions flooded my mind.

Had I made the right decision to apply for this awesome, much-needed promotion leaving my 7-year position as a dishwasher?

How am I going to pay my bills and take care of my son?

I didn't know what to do.

See, your mind can make you feel like you don't deserve better. Yet, the bible clearly says,

"Beloved, I pray that in every way, you may prosper and enjoy good health, as your soul also prospers."

[3 John 1:2]

When I got home, my son, who was playing his game, could see the tears in my eyes. He asked me what was wrong. When I told him I lost my job, he dropped the remote and hugged me. My mom overheard us and came out of her room. She started stomping and praying loudly.

I will never forget it; that was the day my house become a sad structure of concrete, with the sheetrock a hollow space of silence.

I had nothing left in me to fight.

Well, at least that's what I thought.

As the days turned into weeks, the weeks into months, and the months into years, reality kicked in, and I became very stressed. I lost a drastic amount of weight and fell into depression.

There were days I sat on the stairs and just stared. I almost lost my mind.

My house, once filled with groceries, was now empty. The electricity was out for months at a time, and on the top of everything, bank collectors were calling me just about every other day threatening to take me to court and repossess my car.

In my head, I felt like my life was over. Sometimes, I even thought of ending it sooner.

Still, God kept me.

A few months before I lost my job, I had started a nail class that my co-worker had suggested. I'm glad that I did because that was the one thing that would keep me afloat for a while.

Still, even that had a downturn.

My Dad and I tried to stay in touch as much as possible. He passed away in 2012. This was sad because I had just gotten to know him in my pre-teen years. I had really grown to love him and respect him with my whole heart. What I loved about him was that he always encouraged me to get to know his side of the family. To this day, they don't think I'm his child. Still, he and I had a bond that no one will understand. He went to his grave, saying I was his child, and I believed he's proud of me.

In 2013, the bank finally took my car. By this time, I was strong enough to endure it. If they had taken it in 2009, I might not have been here to write this story.

I went from driving to catching the bus and walking in the boiling hot sun. My so-called friends pointed and laughed at me as I walked to work.

My co-workers even made fun of me. One of them also went as far as pretending to be a bank manager telling me to come for my car, only to burst out laughing, saying it was a joke. I had to restrain myself from bursting into tears.

I was hurt, but I tried to keep a smile on my face. I had to stay strong for me.

One day, I decided enough was enough. I needed to stop being a victim and realize that I was victorious. I had to make some decisions that were going to impact my life.

I had been a singer since I knew myself. I decided to use my talent for good. I stayed at the salon as this was my bread and butter at that time, but I also got up, I started looking for positive things to do in my life and with my time. I started focusing on what gifts I had and not what money I didn't have.

I auditioned for a musical and got a spot in the choir. The musical was opera, and my co-workers would laugh as this was voluntary, and I sometimes would have to miss clients to go to rehearsals. They would comment about me leaving work to go to this musical where I wasn't getting paid.

I would just smile as I walked out the door, thinking how some people would never understand that The Lord will use the foolish things to confirm the wise (1 Corinthians 1:27). They couldn't understand that God had a plan for my life, and I couldn't just settle for minor things as it was not my passion. I was determined to make a change.

The musical was a tremendous success, and I felt good. But, this feeling lasted only a short while. Soon, I was back to square one.

One day, I came to the salon, and my spot was occupied by another nail tech. My nail supplies and table had been dragged to the abandoned side of the store. My heart was shattered again. I faked a smile, said thank you and moved on.

Eventually, I started taking my clients at home. Some of them liked it for a while, but soon they began to drift away as they loved and preferred the luxury of the salon. My make-shift, at-home salon, went from having an "okay" clientele to just a few faithful ones that would come from time to time. Sometimes, I had no clients for weeks. Also, my son's father did not bring the child support money

($35 per week) as he thought I would need it to survive. This was true, so both my son and I suffered.

There were many days my son did not go to school because I had no money. I couldn't bear to know he was starving all day at school only to come home still to no food.

Remember I've been there. Many days, I thanked God for my mother and her friend, who provided for her as she would sometimes feed us.

My life was turned upside down, and this up and down motion lasted for the next few years. I had to step back and ask myself what I was doing wrong. I had filled out applications for jobs and got no response.

I had no one.

The only so-called friend I had would count out hundreds of dollars in my front of me, only to make me feel worse about being broke. He'd take me out to eat sometimes and would get extremely upset when I saved food for my son. He was so negative and would often make me feel 'less than' because he had more than I did. He just could not understand the struggle I faced each time I left his company and went back to my apartment.

I knew I didn't deserve this. I knew I deserved to be loved, have abundance, and be happy. I knew I was a good person. I prayed, and I loved The Lord.

Little did I know, God was working on me even at my lowest point.

Remember this: even when our backs are against the wall, He is there giving directions, and shaping our lives. He is there directing our paths. All we have to do is acknowledge Him.

I got tired of being hungry and watching my son suffer. After another failed attempt to get a job, I got on my knees and made a vow to God that I would make a change.

I had overheard a Pastor talking about soul fasting, and I thought I would do that. I went on a soul fast. I cut out food, fake associations, and negativity. I didn't watch television shows that were not in alignment with what I wanted to accomplish. I stopped going places I loved to go, I cut off everything and anything that wasn't in connection with what I wanted to do, who I wanted to become, and how I wanted to see my life. I did not want anything to get in the way of my genuine walk with God. I even made a vow of celibacy for 6 months.

I really meant it this time.

I started reading my Bible once a day. I spent a lot of time reading the book of Job to build my faith. I started listening to motivational music and speakers. I stayed around positive people and let them speak into my life. I cut the negative conversation short and protected myself from gossip. I even blocked numbers. I had made up in my mind to trust the process.

Over the next three months, my life would change drastically.

One day, while in the food store, I saw a lady I met on one of my many unsuccessful job interviews. She had gotten the job and asked me if I got straight. I told her that I had not. In my mind, I had already given up on that job. She told me to come in on Wednesday of that week, and she would help me.

I was flooded with doubt because I had already interviewed for this job and didn't get it. *Why would I waste my time going there again?*

To be honest, I really didn't want to go. I had to remind myself that when you ask God for things, you must do the work to get them. Faith without work is dead *(I then understood the reason I was in the Book of Job).*

So, despite my fear, I went to the place as the lady had directed. I spoke with the Boss, who told me the class was full but to come on Monday to start.

I could have jumped for joy and maybe even slap the roof to express my level of excitement. I smiled so hard that my cheeks felt stuck in that position. I didn't know what to do with myself. This was the first job I had gotten in 6 years.

In my heart, I began to thank God.

The training for the job went on for months, and I was on top of the world. I was filled with high hopes and incredible expectations. Unfortunately, the job shut down before it opened. I would now be out of a job for who knows how long after it took me some years to get this one.

Here I was again, my life flashing before my eyes. I could not bear to take another 2009. At least this time, I was stronger because of my vow to change my life and the fact that I was on my soul fast.

Still, I continued to be strong. Once I got the last salary I made up in my mind, I must find a way to make this money turn over. Yet, I had no idea what to do.

Remember, I was in a musical a few years prior? Well, there was a reunion of the cast, and a friend asked me to write a poem. I really didn't want to, but I did it anyway as I was moving on this newly learned faith.

This poem would become my first book, and that book secured a line of stage plays and other events.

Today, I am an Entrepreneur, Motivational Speaker, and Relationship Coach. I have a non-profit organization that provides for the less fortunate. The list goes on.

Did I mention I now have a stable job that allows me to provide for myself as I continue this journey of growth and success?

Remember, God is a keeper, and when you're at the lowest in your life, lie on your back and look up to Him. You'll see the endless opportunities and some of the most beautiful treasures The Lord has placed on planet earth. Just smile and remember you are one of them.

God has a distinct path for our lives, and you may fall a few times before you can rise.

If you are focused, committed, and trust Him, there is no limit, and the only thing you can do after slamming into the ground is to bounce back up.

Keep smiling, and you'll **Get Over It**!

Sometimes the prayers we have to change others end up changing us instead.

~Dr. Adair

Naeema Finley

Naeema Finley is a passionate mother of two beautiful girls and a dream chaser who owns a natural hair salon in Atlanta, Georgia. She has been in business for over 20 years and has won multiple awards for her exquisite work. Her salon is listed as a "Top 10" natural hair salon in the entire metro Atlanta area. In her spare time, she enjoys consulting and motivating others who want to create business plans to become successful entrepreneurs. Naeema also enjoys traveling the world, is a self-proclaimed "foodie" and enjoys creating vision boards to help plan her business aspirations.

Stick with being the co-pilot and allow God to drive you!!!!

~Naeema Finley

"I Did It My Way…"

In this chapter, I will share with you my journey of becoming the self-actualized, independent, successful businesswoman that I am today. I want my story to serve as a reminder that if you have a dream, then it really can come true if you take a chance. And sometimes those chances are scary, you may feel alone, and you think you can't do it, but you know what? You can…Let me share with you how I did it.

In 2009 I was a hairstylist, married with two beautiful little girls living in my hometown of Las Vegas. It was supposed to be my "dream life," but somewhere along the way, it had become my nightmare existence. The relationship with my husband had become toxic. I knew that for me to live in my truth as my authentic self, I had to leave the situation that I was in. Doing this, however, would also mean that I had to leave the "royalty" lifestyle that I lived in, but deep down inside, I knew that I could get it all back. It just meant that I would have to build a new life for myself "from scratch," but I was willing to take a chance and try it.

During my marriage, I learned that when you marry someone, you are also marrying their background and life experiences. You marry their family, and you marry their values. The way that they were raised affects their lives and how they treat others.

I saw my husband bring all of his "baggage" into our relationship…the positive and the negative. It often blurred his vision, and it was a constant uphill battle for us to have the same vision so we could be on the same page. But we could never get there, and I was miserable. I had begun to lose myself, couldn't walk in my purpose, and stand in my truth. The times that we were on the same page were so limited that I just couldn't take it anymore and that' why I left.

At 36 years old, I packed a 26-foot trailer with the things that I thought were the most important to me and my girls and began my cross-country journey to Atlanta. My best friend helped me to clean out the 3000 square foot home that we lived in with my husband put my 4 and 6-year-old girls in the truck and began the long drive from Las Vegas to Atlanta. I remember that I only had 800 dollars in cash, but I felt rich in my spirit. I was mentally, emotionally, and spiritually rich and that was all that I needed. I was stepping out on faith, and I knew that God would take the wheel and help me drive to Atlanta.

In retrospect, I know that my marriage failed because I felt as though there were more than just 2 people in our relationship. The influence of all the others in our lives was constant and impacted our daily decisions and communication with one another. I'm sharing this because I lived through it. I know it. And I want you to be prepared for it because it can change your mindset and steer you off course from following your dream.

During the time of transition, I knew that I had to change the way that I viewed my world and everything around me. My vision needed to be different because I believed that I had to first change the way that I think before I could change my behavior. I didn't want to do the same things and expect different results because I was alone now. I was a single parent, and my daughters depended on me to "get it right."

So, I started reading self-motivational videos, tapes, whatever it took. There was one particular book and tape that we read and listened to daily. It was called "The Secret," and this book taught us how to "speak what we wanted into existence." Every day my daughters and I would read the book and recite what we wanted in our lives. I created action plans of change that would allow us to move toward our goals, and then we saw positive things begin to happen for us.

I also shifted my religious beliefs. You see, I was raised in the Muslim faith, but as I grew up and began to experience the trials and tribulations of life, I didn't feel that I was connected to it. I no longer felt safe and bonded to it. I recognized that my thoughts and beliefs began to change and were no longer in alignment with the Muslim religion. After a long period of soul searching, I decided to examine and explore a different religious perspective. I then decided to become a Christian.

After 36 years of living as a Muslim, I decided to stop faking what was never meant for me, and I began worshipping Christ. Being a Muslim didn't fill my heart and soul with the strength that I was looking for, so I chose Jesus, and it has been one of the best choices I ever made.

I was so excited about reading and learning from the book *"The Secret"* because it was a faith-based book that I could share with my daughters. I really didn't do that as a Muslim because I didn't feel that in my heart. This time I was teaching and learning, and we were doing it together. It's incredible the things you will learn to do with and for your family. My daughters and I shared a bond, and with that bond, we stepped out on Faith, found a place of worship, and this is what motivated and encouraged us that we could begin a successful new life together.

My Faith helped me to follow my dream of opening my own salon. I found strength in my Faith that I thought I was missing in Vegas. I felt as though it was my calling to move to Georgia, so I was determined to find a safe place for us to live where my daughters could receive a quality education. We settled in a small town outside of Atlanta, and the girls were happy and thriving.

I remember being scared, but it was only a fear of the unknown. Although my sister lived in Atlanta, I really didn't know anyone else, and I didn't know what my new life was going to look like. All I knew was that I was ready to try it. And I knew that I was stronger because of my experiences, so I prayed on it, created my plan of action and then began to execute the steps needed to make dreams come true.

My sister allowed me to rent our first home from one of her investment properties and shared her professional connections with me. Doing this enabled me to work in another salon for about a year when we first arrived. It was a steady paycheck, and I was learning everything I could about Atlanta. I used this time to make stronger connections that I would later utilize to open my own salon. It was hard work and at times, frustrating because I felt as though I was giving my money away to the salon owner. I wanted to be an entrepreneur. I did not want to feel tied and obligated to anyone else. I had done that already in my marriage, and I needed to feel "free."

I had been an entrepreneur while living in Las Vegas, and I knew that this was still my dream. My grandmother in Vegas was a prominent figure in my life while growing up, and she groomed me to become an entrepreneur. She taught me necessary and essential skills to prepare me to be that "boss chick," so I knew that I would reach that goal again in Atlanta.

I didn't want to work for anyone else, so with my determination, I was able to open my first salon within a year of our arrival. It was an all-natural salon that was relaxer free and hair extension free. When I look at it now, I'm not even sure how I was able to do it. Other than my faith, it had to be God. While I never thought that I would fail, I just didn't know if I was really "ready."

However, what I did know was that my dream was to be a successful master hairstylist and open my very own salon. And I was ready, willing, and able to do the work to make it happen. I was not going to allow another person in the world to block any blessings coming my way. I had already done that in my marriage and was not planning to do it again. There was no way that I was going to fail. I remember what that felt like in my marriage and I was not going to volunteer to experience those feelings again.

And guess what?

I did not fail.

After opening my first salon in a year, I opened up a larger location six years later and tripled my clientele. My daughters are consistently doing very well in school, and they are happy. Georgia has been good to us and has allowed me to live in my purpose and stand in my truth.

Sometimes, you have to go through situations to allow you to step out on Faith because where you're at is not where you're supposed to be. I believe in my heart that God will put an amount of pressure on you and challenges that will make you push yourself to not live in fear and to trust in him, and that's amazing.

If you can challenge yourself to believe that God is in control, then you can give it to Him and allow Him to bring your blessings. HE will open personal and professional doors for you and will put people into your path that can help you along the way. He will give you what you need, when you need it and help you succeed in reaching your goals and your dreams. But you have to trust the process. You must trust and believe in God and the plan HE has for you.

Once I learned how to believe in His power, my life has been much more comfortable. I always say to my clients and to my friends, "be careful in what you say and what you do to others because God is always watching you."

I live my life, and although I still have challenges and I'm not perfect, it's a good life. My Faith is stronger than my fear. This is what I needed to push me through the tough times. I stepped out on faith when I left Vegas with just $800 and a dream, and it has allowed me to consistently use it as a stepping stone to achieving that dream. You can do it too.

Yes, it can be a challenge, but you just have to believe, stay focused, and know that what is for you is for you. Listen to your heart and only focus on people who will bring positivity to your life. Know that people will come and go in your life like the seasons, but don't let it stop you from doing what you were born to do. Don't let it deter you from following the dream that God put on your heart.

Leaving my marriage and my husband wasn't easy.

Becoming a single parent wasn't easy.

Moving across the country wasn't easy.

Changing how I worshipped and praised a higher being wasn't easy.

Walking away from a steady income working from someone else wasn't easy.

Falling in and out of love hasn't been easy.

Researching and finding the perfect house for my daughters and me hasn't been easy.

And remaining to myself, my values and my dreams haven't always been easy either.

But you know what? My love, my dedication, and my commitment to the process have never wavered. To "Get Over It, "you have to trust in a higher being...Allah, Christ...whomever. You must stand firm in your Faith and listen to the voices that speak in your ear and fill your heart. It's a fantastic feeling and experience to take instructions from God and know that you are headed in the right direction. I promise you, it will be the best decision that you can make.

Life is good for me now. Wait! Nope, life is GREAT for me now because I learned to trust and believe, and knowing this has allowed me to **Get Over It!** It will work for you too!

Silent tears sometimes reflect the deepest pain but may need the loudest voice.

~Dr. Adair

Dr. LaToya N. Griffin

Dr. LaToya N. Griffin (affectionately known as "Dr. Toy") is a native of Atlanta, GA, and is the mother of one daughter, Ashleigh. She is a STEM Woman with most of her years dedicated to a Fortune 100 Company in Atlanta, Georgia. She is also multifaceted and has several entrepreneurial endeavors, including being a Real Estate Developer & Investor and owner of an Educational Resource Consulting, Customer Service, & Publishing Firm. She is the Founder of Secret Miracles Unlimited Foundation, Incorporated, a Non-Profit, that empowers, educates, inspires, and nurtures tween and teen girls (ages 10 – 19) to become leaders - overcoming any obstacle through mentorship and philanthropy (www.secretmiraclesunlimited.org). She loves volunteering, traveling, the serenity of water, nature, jazz, and spending time with family and friends.

"If I can, she will."

~Dr. Toy

"It is not how you start, it is how you finish."

~Author Unknown

"From Teen Mother to Doctor: Against All Odds - A Secret Miracle"

This chapter will unveil any thought that was ever-present regarding the idea that you cannot overcome any obstacle that you encounter. As a teen mother at the age of 16, Dr. LaToya N. Griffin, affectionately known as Dr. Toy, overcame all odds and became a leader. In this chapter, she tells a portion of her story and provides five points that assisted in her overcoming her obstacle (her *statistic*, as she calls it). Dr. Toy believes that there is a leader in all of us, *and* with drive and perseverance, anything is possible.

The Beginning

I was raised in a Christian household. It was a life that I learned to love and appreciate. Yet, as I became a teenager, I did not have the strength to fight temptation and bad influences. By the time I was 15, I was pregnant.

Yet, my life was not over; it had just begun.

Let me take you to the early years.

My mother and I were always very close. I was born when my mother was 19, and my dad was 17. As life would have it, my mother ended up raising me as a single parent with the gracious and loving help of her sisters and brothers. She always made sure I had the best and worked day and night to provide for me.

It was just the two of us until I was 9. At the age of 7, my mother began dating, and for two years, there was excitement because I had great examples of couples in my family with my uncles and aunts, so that is all I knew, and I was happy that my mother and I was gaining that. I was also excited because my soon-to-be stepfather was very nice to us, and I was gaining two brothers as he had two boys. He also was a veteran, and I was intrigued by that. He smothered my mother and me with gifts (and as a child, of course, I liked that). We would go out as a family, and it was just GREAT! After two years of dating, we became a family, but then…..

Everything changed when they got married. After a while, my stepfather's true colors started to show. He was very domineering and wanted everything to go his way. He started disliking me because I was "in the way." He would discipline my brothers, and even as a child, I knew that the discipline was not right. I was never treated that way physically, but emotionally, I was being torn down.

Things changed once the hitting turned towards my mother. One night, after leaving a basketball game, I overheard my stepfather screaming to the top of his lungs at my mother. Then, I heard something fall. I ran to the room, but the door was locked. I attempted to get in, but I couldn't. Once the door was opened, my stepfather stormed by, my mother was standing in shock and ran to me. We held each other tight as though to never let go. I knew that the only way out was to pray (this is what I was taught).

My mother stayed and really tried to make her marriage work, even though he put us out of the house at least once a month or every other month. My grades started to fall, and I was too young to understand all of this. I visited my uncle and aunt every summer, so I asked if I could live with them because my grades were important to me, and I needed peace so that I could focus. Although it was not easy for my mother and me, it was decided that I should go. I knew my mother loved me and never doubted it once. My mother and aunt talked a lot, which made the move easier. My mother made sure to stay in contact with me, so we never lost our relationship.

While staying with my uncle and aunt, mentally, everything was better. Although my family never missed a beat in loving me, I began to long for missing pieces. At least that is what I thought at the time. Even though my family continuously instilled self-esteem in me, with everything that I had gone through, I was still unsure of myself. This was compounded with me being easily influenced and found myself succumbing to peer pressure.

My friend and I were raised the same way; we came from great families. She was a year older than me, and both families trusting us to be with each other, she became my confidante outside of my family.

We held secrets between us. Because we were trusted, we were able to go out alone to the mall and sometimes the movies. Eventually, we fell prey to our circumstances. At first, we would meet people, but nothing ever materialized; no relationships, nothing other than meeting at the malls. I initially felt it was safe, although I was going against my morals by not being honest with my whereabouts. In my mind, I created an excuse for it and continued to do it for months because it gave me a sense of peace (what I thought was *fun* at the same time).

I never knew and still do not know the root of my friend's decisions to go astray. For me, it was a sense of belonging. I felt so lost, but so secure at the same time. It was a strange time in my life because I was longing for more attention but felt as if I was getting from my family at the same time. I did not realize as a young child and teenager that I was missing the presence of my father. It was strange because my uncles were always there, so I did not connect the need. And, especially during this time, as I was living with one of them. My uncle made sure that I was protected and well taken care of, so the thought or feeling that I was missing something never occurred to me. This was also because my mother shielded me from seeing certain things regarding my father.

My mother would always dress me pretty, and we would have Mommy-Daughter days. We would go to McDonald's, Stone Mountain, Six Flags, Malls, or outings with my aunts. So, I never realized that in some of those moments, she was protecting my feelings when my father was supposed to show up. When he didn't, she covered it with an outing. My mother never spoke against my father and left the door open for him to be in my life. I always knew this because any time I wanted to call or asked to go see him, she was always willing.

As I was preparing for my story to be revealed, I spoke with my mother in 2017 to receive permission and to put together some of my life's puzzle that I was not clear on, which this was one of the pieces. She informed me that she always wanted to protect me and my feelings and never wanted to come between my father and I, so she found a way to do it silently.

In the end, with my father not around most of the time and my stepfather being the way he was, I was still missing a huge piece in my life. My uncles were always there, but *"the piece"* was still missing.

Eventually, I started dating my high school sweetheart.

I spent a lot of time in one of my uncle's and aunt's house because I wanted to spend time with my cousins. One of my older cousins (1 year and ½ apart) and I were very close, like brother and sister. He was very protective of me and sheltered me. When I wanted to hang out with him and his friends, he told me no. But, one day he gave in and finally took me to a party. My Aunt found out, interrupted the party, and took me home. After that, I could not go out anymore with my cousin.

I asked him if I could meet anybody because I was "bored." My friend mentioned she had a boyfriend, and he was very attentive to her; she could tell him anything. My cousin consistently said, "No!" until this one day….

Now, remember, I was still searching for "the piece" of belonging.

He decided I could meet one of his friends (his best friend), and that would be all.

So, we met. We began to date.

Since I was very sheltered, I was not allowed on public transportation during this time in my life. My cousin had a car so he and his best friend, who became my boyfriend, would drive me to school before they went to school. Our "dating" turned into cutting school because when my cousin didn't go to school, I didn't either. (Not a good thing at all, but a part of the story and my truth.)

This was not like me; I was a good girl. Keep in mind, we were all good kids to the outside world because we came from great family roots.

Both my friend and I came up in families where certain things were not discussed. If it came up, we were too embarrassed out of respect for our elders to say anything. So, we confided in each other.

Both of us continued dating for a while, and soon my friend became pregnant. Shortly after that, I also became pregnant.

Oh, my goodness, what would I do?

I was living with my uncle and aunt, and there was no way I would tell them.

No way!!!!

My friend and I would sit on the phone, ponder, and worry.

WHAT IN THE WORLD WOULD HAPPEN TO US?!

In our hearts, although scared, we had to face it and go through with it.

A Teen Mother No One Would Believe

Doctor's appointments and fear; this became my life.

At 15 years old, I did not know what to do. My family did not know, and I did not know how to tell them.

My child's father, my cousin, and I stuck together like glue. It was April when I became pregnant, almost the end of the 10th-grade year. I was able to end the school year without my peers and teachers ever knowing. I was living a secret life and screaming inside.

I confided in another friend because she had a baby the year prior. I figured she knew everything was I feeling. She told me not to worry and told me she would help me tell my aunt.

The plan was that she would tell her mother, and we would all tell my aunt together on a Sunday. However, when she told her mother, her mother immediately called and spoke with my aunt.

When my aunt found out, she came into my room and asked me three times, *"Are you pregnant?"*

Each time until the third time, I said, *"No, ma'am!"*

I was so afraid.

My aunt had lost her baby to a miscarriage, so I did not want to put her through anything else. The third time she asked, I burst into tears and told her I was. She quietly left the room and called my mother.

Before all of this, I knew that both my mother and aunt already knew about it. I thought this because one day (before cell phones), the home phone rang, and I answered in the front room while my aunt picked up in the back. It was my mother. Before I could say anything, my aunt started speaking. So, I listened (ok, maybe I should not have been eavesdropping, but fear was kicking in). I knew my aunt could see my body had changed its shape and that I missed my menstrual cycle. It was then that I heard her tell my mother that she thought I was pregnant.

I am not sure what was said after that because I quickly and silently hung up the phone and panicked. I was terrified.

About an hour later, my mother came over. I opened the door, sobbing and begging for forgiveness. And as I opened it wider, I saw a lime green gift bag with balloons. Mentally, I was perplexed. I did not understand why I was receiving gifts because I had done something terrible.

My Mother, with no anger shown, said,

"We have had our tears, and now you will move forward, and you will become."

I cannot put into words how that made feel. My mother was not condoning what I had done, but she was not rejecting me either. Instead, she was there to support me.

My family decided that I would move back home with my mother and stepfather as to not bring shame to my uncle's and aunt's home. They were prominent people in the community, and we did not want them to suffer because of me.

In moving back home, I knew in my heart and mind that I would not be there long. I did not want my baby born into that household. It was evil, and there was no way that my child would have to undergo the scrutiny that I endured from my stepfather.

I never spoke with my mother about how I truly felt. Then, one day, it all came to a halt, and I didn't have to.

My stepfather decided that he would place my brothers on punishment for the reason that I cannot recall. When I returned from my uncle's and aunt's home, he put me on the same restriction. However, my mother and I didn't know this.

Before my mother left for work one morning, I asked her if I could walk up the street to my friend's house until she came home because I was uncomfortable in our house. She agreed, and later in the afternoon, I got myself dressed and started walking up the street to my friend's house.

My stepfather suddenly came up beside me and screamed about my being on punishment, and I was not allowed out of the house. I explained to him that my mother had allowed me to go. I also told him that since I just moved back home, I didn't know anything about the punishment, and then I continued my way.

At that time, I had no respect for my stepfather because of the things that he had done to my brothers, mother, and I. I did not speak back to him after saying that I would be going because I received authorization from my mother.

Back then, we lived on a gravel road that has since been paved (I'm showing my age). As I was walking up the street, my stepfather ran after me and literally dragged me back to the house. I hit and screamed, but he was too strong for me. This would be the first time he physically hit and shoved me. In my mind, I thought about how it would be his last because I would never allow it to happen again. I knew then for sure that I was leaving.

Keep in mind that I was pregnant, so as I am being dragged, I am praying that my baby is safe. Once back in the house, I phoned my mother quickly to let her know to come home, and I ran into my room.

A short time later, my stepfather came into my room without knocking and sat next to me. I was so afraid. He began to tell me about all the affairs and things that he had on my mother. I didn't understand why he would be telling me all of this. He started to say that I couldn't take care of a baby. The conversation was all over the place. I prayed and prayed and wanted to be out of there so badly.

Then, he decided to go to the restroom, and I quietly ran to use the phone in the kitchen (since he had taken the one that was in my room) and called my cousin. I was fortunate that he answered, and I said, "*Help!*" I quickly started telling him what was happening as soon as I did, my stepfather came out of the restroom and pulled the phone cord out of the wall.

He then pushed me into my room, holding the door so I could not get around him. He yelled to my brother to bring him a belt. At first, my brother refused because he knew how violent his father could be. But, because he was afraid of what would happen to him, he brought the belt.

My stepfather took me by my hand, pushed me on the bed, and sat on my back. I fought and fought but could not get up. He beat me with the belt as I continued to scream, *"I am pregnant, please get up."*

But he wouldn't.

After several hits, he stopped, and I saw on his face the evilest look I had ever seen. He just stood there and stared at me.

By that time, my cousin, his friends, and my child's father arrived at the house. They parked on the street and blew their horns, calling my name. There were about fifteen of them. They never came on the property. Instead, they asked me to walk down.

I jumped up, pushed by stepfather out of the way, ran out of the house. He didn't hold me back because I am sure he figured it would get very chaotic if he did.

Around the same time, my mother arrived, and through my tears, I told her what happened. It was then that she took her final stand. She decided that *enough was enough.*

I told her, *"Mommy, I have to go. I cannot bring my baby into this house."*

She packed our things, and shortly after, she filed for divorce.

Her love for me never once waivered. She had to go through her trials, but when it came to me, she would not stand for it. Until this day and forever, I am grateful because I believe it saved her life.

We moved in with my eldest aunt. After a while, my mother and I were able to move into our own home that was down the street from my aunt.

It felt like heaven, and life felt good, but I still worried about one thing... How could I go back to school pregnant? So, I asked my Mother if I could transfer to my cousin's and child's father's school, and she agreed.

But after thinking about it, I had second thoughts, and, after a few weeks, right before school, I decided that I did not want to go to that school after all. I felt that they were both too overprotective, and I didn't know anyone there. I felt as if I would already be subjected to judgment, so it was best for me to go where people knew me.

My mother would always remind me that the opinions of other people really didn't matter, and no one mattered but her and my family. She told me "life goes on" and made sure that she was positive with me every day.

So, my paperwork was transferred back to my home school. I confided in a childhood friend about the pregnancy. I thought that she would not tell anyone and would support me when school started.

Returning to school was very hard. I started getting looks and hearing snickering. It was hard for me, but I made up in my mind that I had to keep going. I would have to be out in January to have my baby, so I had to work hard and keep my grades up so I could graduate on time. And that was precisely what I did. All the judgment from people made me stronger.

My mother continued to dress me well, and I went to school every day and endured. I began to see a change in people because they realized that I was not typical. I was resilient and a fighter and would not give up. I became very close to two girls, both with their own life trials and obstacles, and we stood together and supported one another.

By the time I was to leave the school to have my baby, I was on the Honor Roll, and ahead of where I should have been. My mother set up a plan with my teachers to get my schoolwork while I was on maternity leave. She was and is the best mother in the world! I completed the assignments, and she returned it weekly for grading.

At the age of 16, I had my beautiful baby girl. This was the start of a new life. It was a long road, but I would stay my course and make it to my destiny.

Life After High School, with a Baby

I graduated from high school at the age of 17, and my daughter was one year old.

After having a college recruiter come to my school and house, I decided to attend DeVry Institute of Technology (now University). I wanted to make sure that I had no break between high school and college so that I wouldn't change my mind.

I opted for a 3 year-round program, so I could finish, start my career, and assist my mother. She was now taking care of both the baby and me. I did not think that was fair, and although we had full support from my daughter's father, his family, and our "village," I wanted and needed to contribute.

My entire mindset was to assist, so a burden could be lifted off of my mother. So, with only a month's break from high school, I started college.

With my family's help, my baby was taken care of. I had long days and nights, and my aunt was my childcare provider. This was such a blessing, as my baby would not have to go to traditional daycare.

Within 3 years, at the age of 20, I graduated with a Bachelor of Science Degree in Business Operations. What a good day!!!!!

After graduating from college, I took a sabbatical and traveled to decide which field I wanted to enter. My family again, very supportive, allowed me to flourish and how grateful I am that they did!

Once I returned, it was time to face reality. I really have a drive and passion for people, so I decided that I wanted to work in Human Resources. However, I did not land a position in Human Resources (HR) as my first position. I was instead hired as an Administrative Assistant with a local box manufacturing company. This allowed me the opportunity to understand the workplace and gain knowledge of day-to-day operations. After a while, I began to *really* have a desire to pursue my HR dreams. So, I started to apply.

At a career fair, I met a recruiter from Wachovia Bank (now Wells Fargo), and she called me shortly after for an interview. I was so excited. I was interviewed, hired, and began working as a Pre-Employment Administrative Assistant. This was such a fulfilling position as I helped people gain employment. I truly loved it!

While there, I decided that I wanted to pursue my master's degree. So, I applied and was accepted into Keller Graduate School of Management. I studied for my master's degree in Human Resource Management. The new millennium (Y2K) was approaching at this time, and under the influence of my family and my desire to succeed for my baby girl, I decided to become a dual-enrolled student and pursue a master's degree in Information Systems Management.

During my studies, I decided that to gain a high-level position, I needed to take a leap of faith and resign from Wachovia. So, I quit without another opportunity lined up. I do not encourage this if you are not prepared, but at the time, I needed to take this step to get where I wanted to be. Funny as it was, I had no clue where that was, yet I knew that if I took one step, God would take two. I had to trust and believe that I would land where I was supposed to be to advance my career.

I began to interview as I continued my studies at Keller. I received my Master of Human Resource Management degree a few months later. The weekend after graduation, I started my IT career and landed a position as a Network Operations Analyst. Shortly, after I completed my classes and received my Master of Information Systems Management.

Upon receiving the 2nd degree, my counselor informed me that I only had 1 more class to obtain my Master of Business Administration (MBA). I knew that an MBA was of great importance, that it would further my career, and if I pursued it, my daughter would be so proud of me, so I completed the class.

My new company was technology-based and was terrific for me. Due to my desire to continue to grow and further my career, I was determined to be the best that I could be. In turn, I climbed the ladder and joined the Leadership Team. (This was a during the time {landed position in 2000} when the IT profession was rarely known to have women and specifically African American women. Although we are still under-represented, the ratio was much less when I entered the field. Girls, if you are reading this.....consider the IT/STEM profession! ☺)

Through my profession, I was able to build my 1st home at the age of 27 (I will forever say "for my daughter" more than myself). Then, after almost 6 years, through a referral, I was afforded the opportunity once again to further my career. I was hired with a Fortune 100 Company in Atlanta, Georgia. As a native of Atlanta, this was huge in my family. Continuing the legacy of my aunt, who was employed at the same company in the 1970s.

Through it all, I had a powerful will to be an entrepreneur, so inclusive of being a corporate professional full-time, I added entrepreneurship. I have pursued everything from Real Estate, Multi-Level Marketing, Business Operations, Customer Service Consulting, Promotions, Publishing to Travel. Above all things, my greatest desire is to serve and assist others.

Through prayer and obedience, I founded Secret Miracles Unlimited Foundation, Incorporated to serve and mentor girls. Secret Miracles Unlimited Foundation empowers, educates, inspires, and nurtures tween and teen girls (ages 10 – 19) to become leaders – overcoming any obstacle through mentorship and philanthropy (www.secretmiraclesunlimited.org).

There is a Leader in All of Us (How to Overcome)

There is a leader in all of us, *and* with drive and perseverance, anything is possible.

I want to share five key points that assisted me in overcoming my obstacles, and I hope they help you.

Work for God and Not Man

Early in my career, around the age of 23, I started feeling that I work from God and not man in my spirit, so I operated in it, and it allowed me to address my day-to-day surroundings in a way that would please God. It was not until later in my life that I realized that this teaching was found in the Bible.

Colossians 3:23, which became my favorite scripture as it says,

> *"And whatsoever ye do, do it heartily, as to the Lord,*
>
> *and not unto men."*

My life: Many times, in personal or professional settings, I have been challenged (challenges are good because they help you grow). Instead of responding in a "fleshly"/human-like way, I learned to wait before responding as to not respond out of emotion so that I could respond and carry myself in a "Godly" way. (The flesh sometimes peaks through 😊, no one is perfect, but with prayer, I aim for calmer and more spiritually directed responses.)

Time Will Move With You or Without You

Time will move with you or without you, so always move with it. Life is forever changing, embrace the change, and evolve with it. Never stop learning as there is always more to be gained.

When you learn and gain more knowledge, reach back and help others that need you and your guidance.

I fought to overcome my statistic. Education was my means to do it. I was intentional in that area. Yet, there was more than that. There was the support that I was given by my family, close friends, and mentors that assisted in my journey.

I could have given up. I could have accepted what society said I would be, but that was not an option. No matter what life throws at you, giving up is not an option. It will not be easy, but it will be worth it. When life gives you lemons, make lemonade.

Life will come, push to overcome, be open and willing to receive support, and in turn, support someone else that may need you.

My life: I made a conscious decision to push to get my education against all the odds because the years would keep passing with or without me doing so. I learned to balance my life and stayed focused on accomplishing my goals.

Once you get into a good habit of life and "living," you will be able to endure, enjoy, and "live" despite anything that comes your way.

Build Relationships and not "Ship Relations"

This pertains to networking and relationships. Building relationships is one of the most significant factors, if not the greatest factor, to create and sustain happiness; and successful life. Always be mindful of the relationships that you build as certain ones can hinder your progress. Stay focused on building solid ones and once you have them, maintain them and not ship them. *Shipping* refers to not being consistent, not being honest, and having the wrong motive/agenda. If you "ship" your relations, it will be difficult for others to trust you, and this may ultimately affect you in the long term.

My life: Early on, due to my situation, and due to fear, I found myself not being honest with my family (remember, I was cutting school and I was not honest about being pregnant).

I could have affected my relationship with my family by not being upfront. As I grew into an adult, I made every effort to be honest, consistent, and communicate. I also learned how to build stable relationships with those attributes, and therefore, I was able to climb the ladder early in my profession. I was trusted to tell the truth. If you do something, admit it, it deems for a better outcome, less stress, and peace of mind. Stay true to yourself.

Genuinely Care and Love People

Your overall purpose is to have a fulfilling life. When you genuinely care and love people, you will attract the same. This means doors will open, not that life will be perfect because that is not reality, but you will attract what you are.

Always remember to attract well by being well. Always love genuinely through it all!

My life: No matter what, I love through it all. We all have short-comings, and it is not for us to judge anyone. Allow people to be who they are and believe them. Focus on your life and how you would like it to be. You may choose for that person not to be in your immediate surroundings, or they may select against you, but love through it all regardless. And, beyond that, care and serve others; big or small; it all matters. We all have a purpose, and there is someone that needs you, and your story will help them. You will attract what you are.

Aim for your Goal, But Never Forget the Angles

Without the angles of preparation and emotions, the process would be easily forgettable. In aiming for your goals, you will have a life experience to carry with you. You will learn and grow from these experiences. Always remember goals with angles equals life experiences. The angles will come in different forms but continue to aim for your goal, and you will achieve it.

My life: My goal was to overcome my statistic of being a teen mother. Therefore, I intentionally prepared myself through education and life to attain my goals.

I had sleepless nights, with lots of reading, studying, researching, applying, and preparation. It was either for class, interviews, or meetings and trust me, I've had every emotion there is ranging from fear to nervousness to anxiety. But each time I pushed through to overcome.

I aimed and succeeded, and so, will you. You must aim!

With any obstacle, you must decide that you will not settle on being in that position. The keyword is "decide." You must decide to deal with yourself internally and not devalue yourself for any reason. Be intentional and choose to overcome any obstacle and accomplish your goals; it can and will be done. In doing so, if you need additional assistance, use these five points that I hope you carry with you as takeaways and help you to *Get Over It!*

God is not the "author of confusion."

We are.

We create our own mess when we want to do it our way and not HIS way.

~Dr. Adair

Jae Haeri

Jae Haeri is an author and speaker who works to help people struggling to heal from trauma, overcome the debilitating feeling of being stuck, discouraged, and exhausted by misery so that they can lead healthy confident joy-filled lives. She holds a Neuroscience degree from Furman University and a Juris Doctorate from Georgia State University. She's a certified life coach with specializations in cognitive behavioral therapy and neuro-linguistic programming. Jae has helped hundreds worldwide, empowering them to thrive in all aspects of life.

"Courage is not having the strength to go on; it is going on when you don't have the strength."

~Theodore Roosevelt

"I'm Not Just A Survivor"

I'm Not Just a Survivor

I'm not just a survivor, I'm a freaking warrior.

I say that proudly.

I didn't just make it through a feat that many, way too many are unable to realize. I fought it, and I won. I'm no longer bound by the fear and shame and guilt of my past. Nor am I defined by it. I owned it. I broke free. I am free.

Here's my story.

He was beautiful, tall, handsome, charming, and sexy.

Here I was, the twice-divorced single mother living a tale of silent desperation in the throes of suburbia, seeking and wanting to share my perfect version of life with a special someone. He found me. He sought me. He liked me, and he wanted me.

I was lucky. I was smitten.

Never mind his shady past and inconsistent explanations. Never mind his inaction and complacency. Never mind his undertones of misogyny. I was different. I could prove it to him. I could make it work. I could over function. I could take care of everything. He was here, in the now, he wanted me, and he was mine.

I held on for dear life and vowed to ride it to the end, not knowing the tremendous price I'd pay for "picture perfect."

It started with a raised voice and an apology. Then, it got nasty.

Just a joke.

I was the butt. Ha, ha.

Then, an accusation. No apology.

Then, threats. And, the stalking.

Then, the names. So many names. Every single name. All the names.

It was my fault, so much my fault, all my fault. I was to blame.

Then, the hitting, spitting, slapping, and bruising.

If only I'd not made him mad. If only I knew how to be better. If only, if only, if only, if only.

I was trash. Just a ho. Just a slut. Just black.

Luckily, he loved me; no one would love me.

I didn't know what love was; I didn't know how to love.

It went on, and on, and on, and on.

Children came, and it got worse. And it went on. It went on.

And then, I stopped. I stopped listening, talking, and caring

And started loving me.

My babies.

My mind.

And, I embraced my God.

I stood up for us.

I protected us.

I left him.

And became the woman I was born to be.

My story is simply self-preservation. I'd tried for so long to save everyone else - my husband, my family, my image - that I forgot to protect myself. The moment I decided to walk away for good was one of total clarity. I saw clearly that he would never, ever change and that his sole priority was never me, never our children, and only himself.

Meanwhile, I'd lost it all. That suburban utopia? Lost in bankruptcy. My business? Shredded. Friendships, family relationships, business acquaintances? Totally undone. At that point of utter dismay, I was broke and alone, except for my children. My strength came in standing up for them, to give them a chance at normalcy, to give them a chance at healthy living. And, that meant getting them away from the web of insanity their father had woven all around us.

The Final Straw

It was a balmy night in the Keys. We'd just arrived and had taken a stroll down to the water, watching the waves crash against the sea walls. We all loved the ocean. It was my peace. Even though I was there with him at his insistence, I was happy for the moment. Never did I imagine that merely hours later, I would be calling the police, packing my children up, and hitting the road, fleeing the insanity that was that man. Our momentary peace was destroyed by another lie, another deception, another attack on our safety.

I cannot describe the fear I felt at that moment, yet, it's been my finest moment to date. I finally stood up. I finally said *enough*. I finally walked away for good. I said NO to him, the years of abuse, manipulation, and control, and YES to myself.

Fire up

The first step to my forever peace was allowing myself to get angry. For years, I'd stifled away the hurt and the pain just to maintain the status quo. We were newlyweds. We made vows. God hates divorce. We had babies. Children need both parents. I believed all those things, so I swallowed my tears and hid behind a smile.

But this time, in the Keys, this last time, I let myself really feel it. He'd threatened the welfare of my children in favor of saving his own pathetic reputation, to keep up optics, and to appear to be a decent person. He threw me under the bus to save face. I was disgusted. I was livid. And I'm one of those that when I get mad, I cry, which to him is an opening for faux sympathy.

"Oh, don't cry, baby. Come here. Let me make it better."

Absolutely not. Dude, you can't fix what YOU broke. I didn't even want him to touch me. I let those tears sear down my face and made him watch. I let him have it. I think my hair even got a little straighter from the heat coming out of my head. Every hurt. Every betrayal. Every cuss word. Every name. Every violation. Every bruise. Every bite. Every wicked, evil touch. It all came seething to the surface, and I wore it like armor. There was no smoothing it over this time. He was gon' learn today.

Look up

In fully embracing my pain, I sought validation.

In the past, I'd hidden behind it using my cloak of perfection. This perfect couple with the perfect love story with these perfect babies, and the perfect life.

To hell with all that. I called a trusted confidante. Together, we dwelled, we stewed, we simmered, we fried, and we burnt the shitastic fuckery this man had put me through to the ultimate char. The level of enlightened furor we reached together matched only the derangement of what this fool thought he was about to get away with.

Not today, Satan.

This was the second step in my healing. Seeking and allowing help and support. I was so mad I couldn't think straight, and as we know, what happens in those moments is that these cowards creep in with seemingly genuine apologies to placate our fury. In our gut, we know they mean us no good. We do. We know it. We know it's not right. It's just confusing. This person is SUPPOSED to want what's best for us, yet they continuously berate, rebuke, and attack us. Keeping it straight in our exhausted, confused minds is hard.

We need a trusted, reliable support team. We need someone we can go to in our fury and trust that despite all the emotion, they will hold our best interests at heart. Our support is not found in our tormentor. We cannot heal in the same environment we got sick. That same twisted smile that's wiping away our tears is the same one that just moments ago, was mocking our pain. We need genuine, trustworthy support, someone who listens without interruption and someone who respects our pain and sits with us in whatever capacity we need for as long as we need.

Luckily for me, my support had been established months before. I'd sought treatment at a local family violence center, so they were very familiar with my situation. I was also a member of a support group. This tribe of sisters was quick to understand with few words needed, sparing themselves from hearing the colorful words I tend to use.

Step up.

The third step in my healing was to not just have a plan but to have someone holding me accountable to actually take the steps needed to keep propelling forward. That night in the Keys, in my fury, I called one of my warrior sisters. When the doubt crept in, as it undoubtedly always will, my girl was like, *"OH, HELL NO. This is what we're gonna do...."*

When my heart and my mind were so shattered, she stood strong for me. She had a plan. I trusted her plan. I followed her plan. I was so overcome by emotion, I honestly couldn't trust myself to do what was in our best immediate interest.

Case in point, I headed south for Key West, instead of north to safety. She called and asked where I was. When I told her, she said as lovingly as possible, "DO YOU HAVE KEY WEST MONEY?? BRING YOUR ASS HERE."

So, that was that. Because she was right. And I wasn't thinking straight. She was there to help me when I couldn't help myself. That help, that support is absolutely essential.

Knowing the precariousness of my situation, it was pretty awesome that I had a safe person and planned the vacation around her location. I wasn't keen on going anywhere with a man that was providing very little financial support and a whole lot of criticism and condescending, controlling nonsense day in day out. Going to the Keys versus anywhere else was a part of a safety plan. I knew I had safe people close by that I could lean on in a crisis.

It's critical to have a safety plan for every scenario and to take steps to act on that plan. Toxic people will use every possible opportunity to their advantage, especially when they think your guard is down. We were going on vacation, but I had my guard held high. I had thought through the worst-case scenario. I was prepared to act. I relied on my safe people to lead me out of the darkness. It saved my sanity. It saved my children. It saved my life. I didn't have to make decisions. I just had to trust the people, and the plan that I knew was for me.

Get loved up.

I'd left before. And I went back. I left again. And went back. And again. And again. And went back.

What was different this time?

The difference is the fourth step in my healing. I totally immersed myself in love and support. Don't get me wrong, the people I fled to before definitely love me, but they didn't get it. They didn't understand the dynamics of abuse. They didn't understand the power and control issues.

Moreover, they wanted to believe he could and would be better simply because he said so. They didn't see him as a master manipulator. They saw him the way he portrayed himself - a wannabe awesome husband and father just leaning on God to live right.

Who wouldn't want that for their loved one?

The problem is that it was more of an illusion than any magician could present. He was so good at illusions, he could've murdered a baby dolphin and made it look Christ-like. He was preserving his image. I was preserving my life. I needed to be surrounded by people who saw clearly through his drivel and could give me the love and support I so desperately needed.

Professionals who deal with this type of person on the regular will call a spade a spade and cut through the nonsense. I'd heard a lot of excuses, validations, blame, and even doubts with regards to my truth.

"No one's perfect."

"Maybe you're the one who needs help."

"He's trying so hard."

"The Bible teaches us to forgive."

"We all have issues."

"Turn the other cheek."

"All relationships have problems."

"He doesn't know any better."

"He was hurt as a child."

I couldn't take it this time. I needed no flying monkeys, shape-shifters, haters, naysayers, doubters, or blamers. I made the decision to leave my entire life behind and head for shelter - a safe place with people who had the training, understanding, and knowledge to help me stand up and heal. That love and support is probably the most crucial piece of the puzzle that has been my healing. I have a large community of people that say, *"I understand, I get it. I will sit with you at this moment and help you heal."*

I cannot emphasize the importance of this support enough. It is absolutely essential to healing from any time of abuse or trauma.

Woman up.

As important as it is to be surrounded by love and support, it is equally important to recognize that you must[T8] be your own hero. For so long, I laid in despair, mourning the life I'd lost and wished for a Savior. I wanted someone to pick me up out of my despair and save me from my suffering.

It just wasn't happening.

Don't get me wrong, I'm a firm believer in Christ and that he died so that we could live free. I heard that[T9] message on Easter Sunday and wondered, what the hell am I doing here? Why was I living in bondage and a slave to fear?

God spoke that word to me, but I still didn't know how to leave, how to protect myself and my children with no money, no income, and no resources.

One fundamental lesson I learned is that God helps those who help themselves. No one was going to give me a handout. No one was going to give me a home and furniture and a job and childcare. No one was going to take my hopes and dreams into consideration and rebuild my life to match. I had to work for it, fight for it, and at the very least, *ASK* for it.

This realization hit me when I was in the shelter, and my advocate suggested that despite my many degrees, my background as a marketing professional, having owned my own consulting company for 10 years, that I get a minimum wage job and apply for public housing.

Now her reasons were valid. I was shattered emotionally. I was struggling just to get out of bed every morning. To take a high-powered position would be intense. But I knew that wasn't the life I wanted for my children and me. I didn't leave a messed-up situation to put us in a messed-up situation. I could do better. I said no to the status quo, and I bet on myself.

Let me tell you, it's been everything but easy. It's been astronomically difficult, to say the least. Yet, still, I rise.

My children are thriving. I'm on a path I'm proud of. I'm far from where I want to be, but I'm even farther from where I used to be. I didn't do it all by myself, but I did it on my own. I stood up, I did the research, I found the resources, and I did the work. God did the rest. I can do all things through Christ who strengthens me, but first, I must do my part.

Let me say it louder, for those in the back: I AM MY OWN HERO.

I wanted better for myself, and I went and got it.

Put some respect on it. And dammit, girl, you can do it, too.

Yes, you are hurting and feel weak and violated and downtrodden, but you are a child of God. He created you in His image, and He is magnificent. What does that make you? You were not prepared to be anybody's doormat. You are royalty. Sit up, stand up, and straighten your crown, Queen.

Pay up.

Now, the final step may seem unnecessary, but the power, the strength, the energy this action puts forth into[T11] the universe is unmatched. You've read this far, and you're like okay, hey, yeah, I got it.

Fire up. Seek up. Step up. Love up. Woman up. Cool. But no, that's not it.

When you're in this place of vulnerability and weakness, it's so easy to just sit and nurse your wounds and think that you're fine now that the storm has passed. I made that mistake before and ended up in an even worse situation. The final step in true healing is to pay it forward - use what you've learned and what you've been through to make this world a better place.

As a long-time business and life coach, I've often heard a saying, we teach what we need to learn. There's so much truth in that. I thought my situation was isolated. I felt so alone. But when we start teaching these lessons, we see the pattern of behavior come to fruition time and time again.

We learn to recognize the signs. We know it's real. There's no speculation. We've got the statistics. We see the reality. We see the same exact same blueprint of abuse in people around the world. In teaching from our experience, in sharing our truth, in speaking out against abuse, we can say confidently, abuse is a systemic disease. That it's not an accident. That we're not alone. And that we're doing the right thing by leaving our abusers and standing up for not only our own rights but the rights of survivors everywhere.

Hundreds of men and women have reached out to me since I've started speaking my truth. They share their own stories of heartache and pain. They're seeking, just like I did. And I'm here to be their love, support, resource, and teacher. I can use my experiences to see them through their own. There's power in that. There's true healing in that. There's validation in that. There's vindication in that.

My ex said that he was embarrassed by my work dedicated to victims' advocacy. It "made him look bad."

Guess what? If he wanted me to speak well of him, he shouldn't have behaved badly. Speaking my truth is power. For way too long, I hid behind that perfect life image. It only served to feed his abuse and starve my soul of the love I truly needed. It only helped to show my children that they deserved little or none. It just taught them to be either a villain or a victim.

I had to break the generational curse. To teach them to be something different, I had to be the difference. And to be able to have touched so many lives along the way is an honor and a privilege. I am humbled that God called me to be this vessel. He's turned my pain into purpose. In doing so, I've undermined all the damage that man tried to do. He wanted to ruin me. I only came out stronger. He's still who he is. That's punishment enough.

Be the change you want to see in the world. I know it seems overwhelming, but trust me. You can do it.

Fire up.

Look up.

Step up.

Get loved up.

Woman up.

Pay up.

You can do it, girl. Yes, you can! I got you. ***Get Over It!***

The advice we give and the lessons we teach should be what we learn too.

~Dr. Adair

Leslie G. Howell

Leslie G. Howell is a new and upcoming author. She has written articles in KIA motors newsletter. She has participated in short story contests in Ebony and Essence magazines. Did a cover story for The Generation magazine and became the Editor-In-Chief of Unity/Umoja newsmagazine at SUNY @ Buffalo, Buffalo New York. She has had the privilege of interviewing Spike Lee, Sonny Carson, and Minister Louis Farrakhan. Ms. Howell is a Certified Medical Billing and Coding Specialist and serves on the Resident Advisory Board of Monroe County Housing Authority. Ms. Howell majored in English and African American Studies. She is the proud mother of two of her own children and two grandchildren. Her only daughter is happily married and living in Atlanta, Georgia. Her only son was the recipient of a Governors Board Scholarship at Bloomsburg University. Ms. Howell lives in the Pocono Mountains of Pennsylvania.

"No weapon that is formed against thee shall prosper, and every tongue that shall rise against thee in judgment thou shall condemn. This is the heritage of the servants of the Lord, and their righteousness is of me, saith the Lord."

~ Isaiah 54:17(KJV)

"It Ain't Over 'Til They Shovel Dirt On You!"

My motivation for writing this chapter is to share some personal events that have altered my perspective on life forever. I want to reach out to you, women and men, both young and old, who believe your current situation is the end-all.

I'm here to give hope to the hopeless, a voice to the voiceless, and power to the powerless. You may have been abused sexually, physically, or emotionally. Perhaps you have gone through a divorce or lost your home to foreclosure. Despite our shortcomings, regardless of what they are, we all have the right to pursue happiness.

I give you my testimony that God Almighty is real and that everything in your life can change for the better, if only you have faith and believe.

I've chosen to use pseudonyms for persons instead of their real names to protect the innocent.

This is my story. This is my truth.

When I walked in the Monroe County Courthouse in Pennsylvania on the morning of February 14, 2008, I was prepared to turn myself in. I thought I had killed my husband!

It was 3:30a.m. when my husband came staggering into our bedroom, talking loudly, thus waking me up. He was ranting and raving about who knows what. I begged him to lower his voice because our son, who was nine years old at the time, was sleeping.

Martin, my husband, was hell-bent on starting an argument that I had no intention of entertaining. He continued going on and on, turning on the top light that was very bright. I was now aggravated and groggy, so I got up.

"Don't tell me to lower my damn voice, THIS IS MY HOUSE!!!!!"

He said while slurring and pounding on his chest.

I left our bedroom to close my son's door so that he would not hear this insanity. His voice escalated every time I asked him to keep it down. My husband and I had been arguing quite a lot lately, and frankly, I was tired of it.

"You don't tell me what to do, THIS IS MY HOUSE!!!" he repeated.

He followed me into our son's room and intentionally woke him up. I was now pissed the _uck off. I went into the room to calm my son down as he was screaming for his father to stop. It was then that Martin pushed me down, and we began to fight.

The male child is always going to protect his mother. It was how he was raised.

My son leaped on his father's back and began punching him. Martin threw him across the room, and my baby boy's head hit the metal-framed bunk bed.

My motherly instinct kicked in, and I ran to the kitchen. I intended to get a knife and stab him. But, on my way down the hall, I saw a shovel behind the couch in my peripheral view. *Who had time to get to the kitchen when the shovel was much closer?*

I grabbed the shovel and went back to the room. When I came in, I could see my son cowering in the corner with his skateboard to protect himself. I screamed for Martin to stop what he was doing. He was intimidating our son. He didn't stop, so I gripped the handle on that metal shovel and bashed him in the head with it.

I did not hit him once, not twice; I hit him three times! Blood was running down his forehead like a water fountain. When he touched his forehead and saw that it was blood running down his face, he freaked out and ran up and down the house screaming,

"YOU CRAZY BITCH!!!!

A calm came over me. I can't explain it.

I advised Martin to call an ambulance so he wouldn't bleed to death. I had split his wig wide open.

The Officers of the Pocono Mountain Regional Police Department were regular visitors to our house. They often asked when we were going to get a divorce. The last time they were called was on New Year's Eve, one month before this incident. I told the police then that if they weren't going to do anything, that the next time he put his hands on me, I was going to handle it.

And handle it, I did!

The police department was quite sexist in that the officers felt that a man should not have to leave his house on the word of his woman or his wife. So, I instructed my son to put on his shoes as we were leaving.

We got into my car, ready to leave when Martin came to the door. The towel on his head was blood-soaked, and he was screaming that he bought the car and would call the police and tell them that I stole it.

I ignored him and drove to a nearby hotel.

The next morning, I woke up early to take my son to school. He insisted we go by the house because, after all, it was Valentine's Day and he had made cards for his classmates.

When we arrived at the house, I saw multiple footprints in the snow all over my front yard. I went in, and all the lights in the house were on, including the television. Martin's shoes and wallet were still there too. I had an eerie feeling that he had bled out and was dead. I searched all the rooms and the closets carefully and fearfully, hoping I did not discover a corpse.

Martin was nowhere to be found.

I drove my son to school and dropped him off. No sooner than he got in the building, he told his teacher what had happened the night before. I received a call from the Principal saying that my son was worried and thought that his father was going to do bodily harm to me.

I decided to investigate myself and went down to the courthouse in Stroudsburg, PA. The clerk at the sheriff's office asked me my name.

I told her, "Leslie G. Howell-Nelson."

She then promptly responded, *"Are you the woman who smashed her husband in the head with a shovel?"* She said this with astonishment written all over her face.

While I sat and waited for an answer to where Martin was, I was secretly being detained while the Pocono Mountain Police department had been summoned to pick me up on arrest charges. When they arrived, I was placed under arrest for aggravated assault, simple assault, battery, harassment, and leaving the scene of a crime.

I was then taken to the magistrate directly to be arraigned. I pleaded my case, claiming self-defense as this was the truth. I was protecting myself and my child. The magistrate released me with an unsecured bail. Later, the charges would be dropped altogether.

About a week later, I began to search for a child psychologist for my son. He was having behavioral issues in school. The first thing the school determines is if the problem came from home. In this case, unfortunately, it did. I had to file a Protection From Abuse (PFA) order and have my husband removed from the family home.

The court had decided there were too many incidents, and my son was caught in the middle of his parents' turbulence. Thus, counseling was recommended for the whole family.

I found an excellent child Psychologist for my son and a great psychologist for myself. My sessions began immediately. I was diagnosed with PTSD Posttraumatic Stress Disorder, Depression, Anxiety, and Panic Disorder.

My husband refused to go to counseling. He said there was nothing wrong with him.

A year or so later, my daughter E (my eldest child) returned home from Atlanta. She was pregnant with my first grandchild. My husband was at home and was still drinking heavily. I won't deny that I drank too, and things had progressively gotten worse than they were before.

The holidays were always a fiasco.

The Christmas season that followed, Martin refused to take our son to his Christmas Choral concert at school. K had been practicing for three months and was understandably upset.

He decided to run next door to our neighbor's house to see if Mr. Donald could take him. Mr. Donald and his wife Emma were reliable and were always there for me whenever Martin and I got into altercations. K had dashed out so quickly that the door slammed behind him.

Martin opened the door and yelled behind him.

"You don't pay no bills here! Who the hell do you think you are slamming doors in MY HOUSE?"

I had had enough, and before I knew it, I snatched the Christmas wreath off the front door and beat him in the face with it.

He said he was going to press charges.

The police had to be called again, and I was asked to leave this time since I was the "aggressor." It was then that I knew the children and I had endured enough. Martin and I needed to get a divorce.

Another incident happened soon after that, where my husband body-slammed our son for asking him where I was? Martin had to be removed from the house yet again. This time, however, the judge ordered he stay away from us for a year.

The sessions with my counselor were going well until she asked me about my childhood. Now the real work had to begin...

1966

I was three years old. It was freezing cold and snowing outside.

My big brother and I were standing in front of our home in Jamaica, Queens, New York, as our mother gathered our suitcases. My grandmother was in her black Chrysler with the engine running. The car looked like the batmobile.

I always thought of my grandmother as a superhero, as she was still there to rescue us.

Grandma came to pick us up, after another bout where my father had beaten up my mother in front of myself and my brother. My father suffered from (PTSD) Post Traumatic Stress Disorder from fighting in the Vietnam War. I would later find out that my father was an abusive alcoholic.

As we piled in my grandmother's car, I could see the bruises on my mother's battered face. Grandma drove us across the Triboro Bridge to her house in upper Manhattan. On the days and months that followed, my mother's face healed, she returned to work, and we searched for a new place to live.

My mother was a first-grade teacher with the New York City Board of Education. At night, she studied for her Master's degree at New York University. Grandma found us a basement apartment in a private house in the North East Bronx on Wickham Avenue.

Brand new houses were being built around the corner on Bruner Avenue less than two blocks away. It was a new middle-class neighborhood called The New England Home Owners Association. It would later and forever be known as 'The Valley.'

The year we moved into our brand-new house on Bruner Avenue, I was four. The house we moved into, unbeknownst to me, was purchased by my grandmother.

The new house smelled of fresh paint and cut wood. The floors were shellacked and shiny. It was a two-story brick family house with a fully finished basement, and we had a lot of birthday parties there.

On the weekends, once a month, my mother would have card games and fried fish dinners. My brother and I were the entertainment. We danced and imitated moves from The Jackson Five.

My brother and I made friends with the other children in the neighborhood. I always had this uncanny feeling of inferiority because most of the kids on my block had a mommy and a daddy.

I can honestly say I only remember seeing my father three times in my life.

The time I remember most was when my father came to our new home in the Bronx to visit us. I was five or six years old by then. I cherished being pleasantly surprised and so proud to introduce him to all my new friends. I wanted them to know that I had a daddy, too, even though he didn't live with us.

We owned a floor model Magnavox Television that housed a radio as well as a 33-inch vinyl LP record player.

On the day that my father came over, he and my mother enjoyed music by Nat 'King' Cole and Otis Redding while they reminisce and had cocktails. They were laughing, hugging, and kissing.

Before long, they began to argue, and their voices went from cooing to cussing. My father wanted my mother and us back in his life. My mother must have said no. Furniture was being pushed around, along with my mother.

My heart sank, and my dream of "Happily Ever After" turned into a nightmare!

I realized that the same thing that had happened back in Queens on that dreadful snowy night was happening again here in the Bronx.

Things were being tossed and thrown around until my mother picked up a glass fruit bowl and smashed my father in the face with it. My father's face was cut and bleeding. This time the police had to be summoned.

A black and white squad car with its red, white, and blue flashing lights had been dispatched to 2812 Bruner Avenue. The two white officers promptly manhandled and handcuffed my intoxicated father. Then they tossed him in the back of the police cruiser.

I didn't realize it then, but it would be the last time I would see my father alive. He passed away from cirrhosis of the liver four years later.

As for the broken childhood that my brother and I experienced, my mother and grandmother made sure that we didn't want for anything. We were given the best educational opportunities. They enrolled us in a private Montessori school in Mount Vernon, New York.

Our school bus picked us up in front of our house, while the other children in our neighborhood caught the bus on the corner. Along our bus route, we picked up Robin G., a current actress that was previously married to famous Boxer Mike T. Some of our other classmates and friends were Liza A. and four of the daughters of El Hajj Malik El Shabazz, otherwise known as Malcolm X.

My grandmother was a seamstress and a Real Estate Entrepreneur. She owned five houses. She spared no expense in the things we needed and wanted.

I was enrolled in several dancing schools. The Dance Theatre of Harlem was my favorite. I performed my recitals at The Savoy Manor Ballroom on 149th Street in the Bronx. I loved the fittings, and the custom made costumes. It made me feel like a celebrity. I studied classical Ballet on Pointe, Tap, African, and Modern Dance.

I also attended Barbizon school for modeling. My mother believed in teaching her children about their culture. We visited the same places that tourists came to New York to visit. We enjoyed Broadway plays, museums, The Circle Line, Battery Park, Central Park, the Bronx Zoo, and the Apollo Theatre, where we got to see James Brown, 'The Godfather of Soul' perform. We even climbed to the torch of Lady Liberty (back when that portion was open).

Every provision was made to advance us educationally and financially. The fact that we did not have a functioning father in our life did not deter us.

My mother eventually remarried. I became a big sister. My life changed.

UNSPEAKABLE HURT

I free my soul and give voice to the twelve-year-old girl who was silenced so long ago.

In my twelfth year of life, I was diagnosed with pneumonia. I was hospitalized for close to a month. I clutch my chest now as I recall how much I would cough and the non-stop vomiting that plagued my daily life.

I was eventually admitted to Parkchester Hospital in the Bronx. I lived inside an oxygen tent. I thought I was going to die. I had already missed most of my sixth-grade school year and had to do homeschooling for a while.

My grandmother volunteered to take care of me since mostly she worked at home. Grandma made homemade soups and honey lemon tea concoctions. She made me feel really special and loved. On many occasions, I would stay with my Godmother Eve, who took care of me, and I had three Godbrothers who looked out for me as well.

Grandma's husband was my step-grandfather. He was retired and spent most of his time in the basement watching television and drinking Gordon's gin. There were times when my grandmother had to run errands and make deliveries to her customers. At those times, I would be left alone with my grandfather.

The unspeakable hurt started with him telling me to come downstairs in the basement to watch television with him. Then we would play bartender. Initially, I was the one doing the pouring. Until one day, he told me to take a sip of gin. It tasted horrible, but after a few sips, I started to feel dizzy. He would have me drink it down fast. It was the beginning of my alcohol dependency and the end of my childhood innocence.

One day my grandmother went out, my grandfather wanted to show me his secret collection of magazines. They were Playboys, Hustlers, and the like. He told me it was a secret and I couldn't tell anyone. There were nude images that I had never seen before, and it scared me. He said that if I told anyone that I, *not Him,* would be punished. The worst was that he had me believing my mother and my grandmother would not love me any more for what I had done. He said, who would believe me over an adult?

I never told another living soul.

Each encounter that I had with him advanced from looking at his private parts to actually touching him. I was given more and more alcohol each time. I was getting drunk and passing out. He told me that the reason he was doing this was to show me what boys would do to me when I got older. He said he was going to show me the proper way to do these things.

I was terrified. It went from molestation to rape by the time I turned thirteen.

I carried a tremendous amount of guilt inside me. I thought I must have caused this awful thing to happen to me. I felt like damaged goods and that no one would ever or could possibly love me.

During this time, I began drinking the liquor from the bar in my basement on my own and had discovered other drugs as well. I needed them to dull the pain and fill the gaping hole that I felt inside.

In my teen years, I began to fight a lot. I had a terrible temper and found myself in the Principal's office more often than my mother or I liked.

As a student at Michelangelo Intermediate School, my first fight was with a girl in my class in the seventh grade. She had written something derogatory on the bathroom wall about me, and I whooped her ass for it.

I got suspended from school for ten days. I was a good student, academically, but my behavior was out of control. My mother told me if I didn't get my act together and soon, she was going to send me to my grandmother's house to live.

The thought of that consequence was not an option for me. I got myself together and concentrated on my books. I graduated from Michelangelo in 1976 and went on to Truman High School.

Truman High School was brand new, and we thought it was a country club in comparison to Evander Childs and Roosevelt High schools. In my first year, I got into cutting class and going to hooky parties in the Valley, Boston Sector, and Co-op City (section five). I began drinking Wild Irish Rose, Night Train and smoking weed regularly.

By far, I was my mother's most difficult challenge. She couldn't understand why I was misbehaving so much. I stayed on punishment otherwise known as 'The Rock". I had no idea how to make the unspeakable hurt go away. I was getting high so much that I had pushed the memory of the violation way down deep inside myself.

I was responsible for taking care of my younger sister, and I protected her. In fact, I would make sure that she didn't go to my grandmother's alone because I knew what a monster my step-grandfather was. I didn't want what happened to me to happen to her.

I began dating at this time. Christian B. was my first boyfriend. We broke up when he tried to have sex with me. I was a fun girl who was still afraid of boys. I spent a lot of time in the Valley park playing handball and riding my skateboard across the basketball courts. I had a huge crush on a guy that was much older than I was, but he didn't even know I was alive. He had hazel eyes and a smile that charmed ALL the girls. He was FOINE!!!. I did, however, start dating another boy when I was sixteen.

Darrin M. was his name. A high school basketball star with a mini bike that I loved riding on the back of. My mother didn't care for him. She was afraid I would lose my virginity to him. She was right and wrong. He was the first boy that I was intimate with, true. But my virginity had been snatched away by her stepfather like a thief in the night. I remember my grandmother telling me, "All boys want to do is get into your pants." I wanted so badly to say to her what her husband had already done to me. But, I was afraid I would lose her love forever.

During this time, my grandfather had a stroke and had to be placed in a Nursing home. I thought to myself that finally, God had heard my prayers. I even prayed that he would die there. He did die there, eighteen years later.

The irony of this was that I had to be the person to claim his body at the morgue. I wanted to send him straight to Potters Field (a cemetery in New York) in an unmarked grave. My favorite Aunt T advised me to do the right thing, which was to give him a decent funeral. She said if I did, this God would bless me. I did, and God is Blessing me right now.

I was still a rebellious teenager. I had even tried to run away from home with my next boyfriend, Barney J. He was in the Army and had just gotten out of boot camp. I figured if we married, I could get away from New York and go live with him in Missouri, which is where he was stationed.

I was willing to take the chance.

I packed my things in a suitcase and headed for the door until my mother said: "where do you think you're going with my suitcases?" I went back to my room and shoved everything I owned into two shopping bags. Then I went to my good friend Shell's house. She gave me car fare so I could meet up with my beloved BJ in section five. My mother found out about my planned escape and beat me like a stranger in the street!

I was on 'The Rock' for another six months. She stopped all his phone calls and intercepted his letters.

My mother had come to her wit's end with me and took me to see a Psychiatrist. I went because I was forced into it, but I still refused to tell anyone what had happened to me.

My life went on, and I graduated from Truman High School. I attended John Jay College during my first year, but I hardly went to class. I still felt lost in the world.

My older brother was already a student at the University at Buffalo. My mom thought it a good idea for me to get out of New York City and go to a school where my brother could keep an eye on me. I was grown and didn't need looking after, or so I thought.

It was my first time being away from home on my own, and I loved it. I decided to actually give my academics an opportunity and prove to myself that I was worthy of being there. I was involved in the Black Student Union and became a Sigma Dove (an auxiliary of Phi Beta Sigma Fraternity Incorporated).

I became more interested in my writing and wrote a cover story for *Generation News Magazine* on campus. I absolutely loved writing, and I had finally found my place in the world. I continued my studies and decided to major in English and African American Studies. I loved the positivity I felt in Buffalo. I had even gotten engaged in a Sears parking lot to Samuel N., although we did not marry.

A few years later, a group of students and I founded *Umoja/Unity News Magazine*, which was a collaborative effort of all the minority students. I had been offered an internship by the African American Studies Department at the *Buffalo Challenger*, which was a local African American Community Newspaper.

I became the Editor-In-Chief. We interviewed Louis Farrakhan, Spike Lee, and Jesse Jackson, just to name a few.

That same semester, my line sister Romunda H. and I were at a sorority conference in Pittsburgh, PA, when we became Gammettes. The international Grand Basileus (Head President) charged the two of us to recruit young ladies for Sigma Gamma Rho Sorority Incorporated in Buffalo. I, Romunda H, Melissa D, Lisa J, Sheila A, and Fatima P. founded Kappa Pi Chapter with the assistance of our Dean Theresa B., I was the chapter's first Basileus (President).

We did a lot of community service and worked with the youth and seniors. Our chapter received awards and accolades in recognition of our work in the community. I was honored with the most prestigious award bestowed upon an undergraduate, 'SIGMA OF THE YEAR.' I was also awarded a plaque for bringing the Unity newsmagazine into fruition.

I met my daughter's father in college. He was a drummer, and I was a dancer. We stayed together for nine years. The greatest gift he ever gave me was my precious baby girl.

I started to feel like I had a purpose in life. Those horrible memories were behind me. Who was I to drown in self-pity when there were so many others who didn't make it, while others still needed encouragement to go on?

By the time I graduated, I felt like I had finally made myself and my mother very proud.

In the fall of that year, my mother passed away, and I was devastated. I had been appointed the Executor of her estate and became a landlord of five properties overnight.

I handled the family business.

Education had always been a priority in my house. I had to ensure that my younger sister graduated from High School (at the time she was still a minor). I made sure she went on to college. She received a Bachelor's Degree in Psychology. My children both attended college, as well. My son even received a full-ride scholarship to Bloomsburg University.

My daughter is happily married and living in Atlanta, GA, with my two grandchildren.

Currently, I am divorced and living my life to the best of my ability. I lost my home to foreclosure after 18 years of marriage. My son and I were homeless for nearly two years.

I am still striving for peace and happiness. I've even found love again with N.R., a man from the neighborhood whom I had a crush on so long ago. He has loved, challenged, and encouraged me. (You know who you are).

I am fortunate to be pursuing my dream as a published author. I am ecstatic, and I am grateful to God.

As I look back on my life, I know I am truly blessed because I am six feet above the ground and still breathing. It is my testimony and my purpose. Everything that I went through in my life was allowed to happen for me to reach this place and moment in time. I pray that my experiences will help someone else. It has been a struggle, but it has made me a stronger woman.

Faith in God was vital in my writing. Forgiveness was essential. It was hard at first, but I did it. If therapy is needed, get some help. There is no shame in it. If you want to go back to school, do it. Persevere, I made it through, and so can you. I want to thank J.C. for helping me with this story and always being there for me.

Don't be afraid to fight back! Don't be scared to allow yourself to **Get Over It!**

The Life Strategies that helped me to Bounce Back:

1. *I pray every day and read scripture out of the Bible when I awake.*
2. *I placed positive affirmations all throughout my house to keep my energy positive.*
3. *I found out about local resources for women and children; there are shelters and programs available.*
4. *I kept my essential documents close and in a safe place.*
5. *I read books by T.D. Jakes, Joyce Meyers, Juanita Bynum, and Iyanna Vanzant'*
6. *I forgave myself for the things that happened in the past. I asked God to help me with forgiving others who hurt me.*
7. *I made amends to the people that I hurt.*
8. *I forged a stronger relationship between my children and myself.*
9. *I addressed my addictions through self-help groups.*

10. *I gave up thoughts of revenge and put the past where it belongs...In the past!*

REFLECTIONS

1. What would you do if you were being abused?
2. Are you in a toxic relationship?
3. Will you leave to protect yourself and your children?
4. Do you have a plan in place?
5. If you need to get away, do you have a friend or relative where you can stay?
6. Getting counseling is not a stigma that it used to be. Get some if you need to.
7. Are you ready to start living a peaceful life?
8. Are you ready to work on being the person that God designed you to be?

The word "NO" really is a complete sentence. Explanations are not needed.

~Dr. Adair

Tamiko Lowry-Pugh

Tamiko Lowry-Pugh is often referred to as "The Empowering Diva," as a voice for Women's Empowerment. She is the CEO of EmpowerME! Life Coaching & Consulting - personal development & lifestyle enhancement firm for women, the CEO of Still Standing Publishing - a Book Publishing Company that publishes memoirs and self-help books and the founder of The Still Standing Alliance – a nonprofit organization that focuses on domestic violence awareness, advocacy, and prevention. Tamiko has constructed a powerful movement dedicated to the empowerment and personal development of women across the world. She is a compassionate mentor and friend, an enthusiastic leader, and a visionary. As an International Bestselling Author, Empowerment Speaker & Coach, and Domestic Violence Expert, Tamiko believes that empowerment comes from within and can be achieved by honoring yourself, your values, and expressing your talents and gifts.

"Stand strong by realizing your vision, understanding your calling, overcoming your obstacles, and pursuing your passions."

~Tamiko Lowry Pugh

"I'm Still Standing!"

I remember, on several occasions, being choked until I almost passed out. Thinking to myself, I'm about to die. My abuser beat me with words, he beat me emotional, he beat me mentally, and he beat me spiritually until I became a broken soul. But the most horrific incident was the day that I decided to leave. I woke up alone, in a state of confusion and panic, helplessly lying in the middle of Interstate-85. Just hours before, I had made a decision. I was finally going to leave my abuser.

As I drove down the interstate, he sat in the passenger seat and threatened to kill both of us if I left. The next thing I knew, he grabbed the steering wheel, forced the car onto the side of the highway, and proceeded to beat and strangle me to the point of unconsciousness. Thankfully, someone saw what happened and called the police. I thought for sure I was going to die on that day. My life flashed before my eyes. I made it out, but not everyone does.

Starting my life all over again was very scary. I was a single parent, working a part-time job, barely making enough money to pay my bills and feed my children. There were so many doubts, fears, and uncertainties. Did I make the right decision to leave my 7-bedroom home? What if I get evicted? Where was our next meal gonna come from?

There were days when I would steal my coworkers' lunches from the break room to take home and feed my children. Things got so bad that one time, after an employee cookout, I stole a huge (unopened) 100 count box of hotdogs that were leftover. My children and I ate off of those for almost a month.

I can also recall a time when I did not have any money for food or gas. My gas tank was almost on empty. It was a Sunday morning, and I really wanted to go to church, so I decided to take the chance and drive to church on an empty tank.

As I sat in the pews listening to 'the word,' I began to cry out to God, asking for "help."

Then, out of nowhere, a man sitting next to me [whom I had never seen before] handed me $20. He said, *"God told me to bless you with this."* Keep in mind, I never saw that man ever again. He must have been an angel in disguise.

During that first year, I had been evicted (not once, not twice) but three times.

For the next few years, I cried out to God to give me an answer as to *why* I had to go through these painful hard times. Why me God?! Why me? Why did I have to go through an emotionally physically abusive marriage? Why God? *Why me?*

I remember sitting in the church pew, asking God, "why me? My pastor was preaching a sermon on turning your pain into purpose. "God didn't deliver you from that abusive relationship for nothing." He said. "There was a reason behind it." "There is purpose out of that pain." It was one of those moments when you think they are talking directly to you. He was preaching from Romans 8:28, *"And we know for those who love God all things work together for good, for those who are called according to his purpose."*

At that moment, I knew my purpose in life. Tears began to flow as I thanked and praised God for turning my pain into purpose. My wounds now became my wisdom. The wisdom that I would share with thousands of women around the world who were going through what I went through.

Now, I know my purpose in life. What do I do next? How do I accomplish what God said I'm supposed to do? How will I reach these women that God said I'm supposed to help? One day God spoke to me, he said to start a nonprofit organization. Through this organization, you are going to help thousands of women. They will look to you for guidance and direction. I thought to myself, really God? How am I supposed to do this?

What will I call it? Who is going to help me? I don't know anything about starting a nonprofit organization or a business. I felt God speaking to me, saying, "Just do it!"

Trusting God and living according to Romans 8:28 has helped me to take my first steps on my path to survivorship, financial independence, and living an empowered life! I now had a name for my organization. The Still Standing Alliance. But, I still didn't quite know where these women were going to come from that I was destined to help. So, with social media as a resource—I began to promote the Still Standing Alliance.

Every day I would submit a morning meditation or something inspirational to empower the people that visited my pages. I also posted domestic violence information and statistics that I felt would be beneficial to those who were going through domestic violence. Likewise, noting inspirational wellness tips for those who were working their Will of Survival plan. Some were so inspired by my postings that they began to call me the *'Empowering Diva'* [which is now branded as of my business]. Needless to say, as a result of social media promotion, both The Still Standing Alliance, and I currently have thousands of followers, which has afforded me many opportunities.

The realization and manifestation of my destiny came when I least expected. I began to get requests for paid speaking engagements, community partnerships, and media appearances. I met the love of my life and remarried. Not long after that, I was able to leave my job in Corporate America and work my passion and purpose full time.

Everything that we go through in life has a reason, a purpose, and a lesson. Being able to understand the lesson and make it my life purpose has given me the strength and courage to live and to love again.

No matter what your situation may be, no matter what it is that you are going through, it will eventually work together and become your purpose. I have learned to view every wound as an educational assignment. Whatever it is that you go through, always ask yourself, What's the lesson in this? Was it to make you stronger? To learn how to trust your instincts? Or, simply to forgive. Whatever that lesson maybe, learn from it and never look back...that's how you ***Get Over It!***

Asking for help doesn't mean you are weak. It just means that you need help.

~Dr. Adair

Nicole Morris

Nicole Morris is an avid believer of Jesus Christ, mother of two boys, educator, and entrepreneur. Nicole was born in Boston, MA, and currently resides in North Carolina. She received her Bachelor's degree from the University of Massachusetts- Amherst in Psychology/Communication and later obtained her Master's degree in school counseling. As a 10-year veteran, she has taught in various positions throughout the education profession, ranging from a physical education teacher to currently serving as a middle school counselor. Her expertise includes parent involvement, social-emotional learning (SEL), and young adult advocacy. She thrives on impacting future generations through the implementation of 21st-century education and assisting with the discovery of unrealized purpose.

"Life has a way of preparing you for a glorious eternity."

~Nicole Morris

"Letters from an Undisciplined Disciple"

This chapter is a compilation of journal entries written throughout my adult years. Each entry provides readers with in-depth insight into a significant past, present, or future event I experienced. My goal is to empower the lives of the readers by sharing my "rock bottom moments" and provide a practical approach to overcome any obstacle. Ultimately, my faith and relationship with Jesus Christ served as the determent factor to the supernatural abundance I experienced. Come join me as we journey through the adventurous life of an undisciplined disciple.

January 1

Dear Self,

"Whoever loves discipline loves knowledge, but whoever hates correction is stupid."

Proverbs 12:1, NIV

Discipleship is a life-long process of servitude and commitment. A metamorphic state of being that requires a consistent, intrinsic motivation to obey the voice of the Lord. Coupled with the willingness to deny every barrier created by "self" and the agility to confront situations as they arise. An honest evaluation would yield an unwavering trust in God and a conducive loading dock for the promise.

As far back as I remember, I was always different! Even in my baby pictures, I had the appearance of a child uniquely created and the countenance of a distant stranger in search of my real home. Have you ever considered the time, space, and place you operated in were allotted for a specific purpose?

Often times, we lose the ownership of the "promise" or the desired outcome amid the process. This process or journey we call "life" is equipped with an onslaught of tests, opportunities for rapid expansion, and repeated calls to respond. Respond in a way that is effective, uniform, and disciplined. The discipline that speaks to the formalized training, higher-level application, and practical measures which yield sustainable results. Results, if not careful, leads one down a windy road of destruction and deposits your fragmented remains into the dark hole of stagnation.

Stagnation.

A destination located at the foot of the mountain void of the directive "be thou removed, and be thou cast into the sea" and the belief of the promise encapsulated in your heart. Ultimately, our personalized promise is abandoned, recycled for future usage, or delineated to a mere praise report for an unsuspecting recipient.

On the contrary, since "His divine power has given us everything we need for a godly life through our knowledge of him who called us by his own glory and goodness" (2 Peter 1:3), it's imperative to uphold a standard which commands the "promise." Even if we become disillusioned or discouraged, our intrinsic nature is conditioned to thrive. Disciplined in a manner that renders optimal results.

May 8, 2011

Dear Self,

"The end of a matter is better than its beginning, and patience is better than pride."

Ecclesiastes 7:8, NIV

Finally, my journey to North Carolina is complete! The sixteen plus hours of stop and go traffic, periodic visits to repugnantly decorated rest stops, and my inability to recuperate from sore areolas derived from breastfeeding served as humbling mementos. Armed with my best friend and my two young boys, we optimistically journeyed to this unfamiliar territory. The mere recognition of the sign which read, "Welcome to North Carolina: Nation's Most Military Friendly State," ignited a tapestry of emotions constrained deep inside. Today was synonymous with an adopted child meeting their biological parents for the first time. Finally, I arrived in the state resolved as "home" without any expiration date on site.

Months before this automotive trek, I was coasting at the peak of my mountain. As a recent convert back to the Christian fold, I was decreeing and declaring miracles that were manifesting before my very eyes. Attendance in Sunday morning services was a part of my weekly routine, and bible study classes were a non-negotiable towards the development of my faith. Everyone around me knew there was an imminent shift because of the drastic change in my wardrobe and the consistent refusals to "hang-out" in the familiar spots. I was determined to live a life worthy of my inheritance and refused to let anything stand in my way.

Additionally, from a professional standpoint, I was deemed "A Money Making Educator" due to my residency status in one of the academic hubs in our nation...Boston, MA.

At my leisure, I tended to splurge on expensive endeavors such as high-end retail therapy, a plethora of recreational events, and many miscellaneous buys. Despite living under the comforts of my mother's roof, I acquired a fixed mindset which upheld my standard of living at a fraction of the cost.

Most importantly, I had an entourage of family members (parents, aunts, adopted relatives, etc.) willing to provide 5-star child care at a moment's notice. This bonus feature helped ignite a passion for travel and allowed me to travel to several foreign territories. Translated into Layman's terms, "All was well, and there was no need to fix it!

Interestingly enough, weeks before any decisions were finalized, I felt an internal shift to relocate but was oblivious to be the next destination. More often, I found myself making comments such as, "I am beginning to think there's more to life than this," "I'm ready to a responsible mother" and "This place has nothing to offer me." It was evident my time had expired, and I was occupying a purpose space reserved for another vessel. Working was becoming more and more monotonous and the hopes of being laid-off my main desire.

Sometimes, all we need is a catalyst to awaken the dormant purpose resting deep within us. In sync with my metamorphic emotional state, a good friend of mine planted the seed of an opportunity to visit her older female cousin. Since her cousin and I conversed a few times, and our boys were close in age, it made sense to visit her home in the South. After several correspondences, we agreed to a child-free, week visit inclusive of lodging and food to explore this new region...Or, so I planned!

December 18, 2011

Dear Self,

"Many are the plans in a person's heart, but it is the Lord's purpose that prevails."

Proverbs 19:21, NIV

The feeling of everything coming together feels so serene! After a few months of financial turbulence, I am now able to provide my family with shelter, food in my refrigerator, safe child care, and most important- health insurance. Personally, my last full physical exam occurred during my pregnancy close to a year ago. Even though my current health benefits are not extensive, the mere privilege of taking my family to the doctor's was long overdue. Two days ago, the boys and ventured to spend the first part of the day at the doctor's office.

Before the transition, I had not experienced such a high level of lack of co-dependency. There was always a surplus in our home, and the needs defined by Maslow were consistently met. As a matter of fact, I enjoyed serving as a giver and sought to support various endeavors. At this point, my unemployment is terminated, and an extension to funding is not an option. Even though I have not established residency, my children are covered by the state's funding, and the free clinic is located close by. This change in status helped me to embody the words of India Arie, "It's the little things and the joy they bring."

Today was pretty basic. I conducted my daily resume submissions, headed to the neighborhood shops to purchase a few Christmas gifts, and performed a "deep holiday cleaning" throughout the house. Growing up, I always enjoyed this time of the year and being in the presence of family. Unfortunately, my parents were not able to visit because my mom feels fearful because of air travel, and my dad wasn't talking to me. So typical! While we were out, I received a message from my doctor's nurse and made a note to give her a call back later in the day. Once the boys and I got home, we settled in for a night of gift wrapping, cheesy Christmas movies, and a tub of store-bought chicken.

As I entered my room to get the packaging tape, I heard the phone ring and ran to pick it up. I just knew it was "my boo" since he had the day off and called periodically to check on me. When I reached the phone, I quickly looked down and spotted the doctor's phone number flash across the scene. I had forgotten to call them back, but what was the urgency to connect? With a bit of uneasiness, I answered, "Good evening, this is Nicole…"

At this moment, I concluded, my life will never be the same. To be honest, it feels like receiving a life sentence without an attorney and the guaranteed collection of my DNA. Hopeless. The conversation ended with me in a weak position, face down relying on a set of ineffective tear ducts. I was speechless and numb! In an instant, every positive memory stored throughout my cortex was thrust into my limbic system.

I am feeling befuddled because of my undisciplined lifestyle.

March 4, 2015

Dear Self,

"If we claim to be without sin, we deceive ourselves, and the truth is not in us. If we confess our sins, he is faithful and just and will forgive us our sins and purify us from all unrighteousness."

I John 1: 8-9, NIV

Today was the second most prolific experience of my life! The first was becoming the mother of my handsome boys. Even though my birthing process was comprised of two pregnancies, the four years represented evolution and growth in my role as a mother. I remember at the tender age of 24, having the determination and laying in the hospital bed and witnessing the sheer joy smeared across the face of my mother as she scurried around the room. Since this was the birth of her first grandchild, she conveniently devised a plan to accompany me in the delivery room and opted to cut the umbilical cord. Meanwhile, my son's dad appeared to be in a state of shock. It was evident, he missed the culminating classes of sexual reproductive, where the teacher shared about the journey through the birth canal.

Alternatively, two days before my 28th birthday, I exemplified the maturity of a caretaker and secured in my beliefs in "the natural birthing process." My second baby was scheduled to make a grand entrance at a birthing center. The months of planning and distant trips to the center resulted in an emergency delivery at the adjacent hospital. Even in utero, my strong-willed offspring managed to defecate in his sac and sabotage his spa-style debut.

On this day, I admitted to a group of close friends that I was resentful about my role as a parent. Yes, I said it! For the first time in the history of parenting, I revealed the driving emotion which governed my five-year term while in office. Feelings of bitterness, anger, abandonment, and fear sprang forth from the previously planted seed of rejection. I felt rejected by everyone around me and refused to contain it any longer. At that moment, I sought to reclaim my identity and embraced the liberation of being "mom." After the great reveal, I was confronted by an onslaught of blank faces. No one muttered a word. The lull of conversation was broken with comments about the upcoming school break, never to be explored again.

During my quiet time, I reflected on my disclosure. Why had I suppressed these emotions for so long, and what was the root cause of this emotional tapestry? How and why did I move here?

Interestingly enough, this uncharted region served as a pleasant alternative to the emotional dissonance and shame abandoned back home. There I was known as the "Single mother of two young children" whose fathers' statuses varied depending on the narrator at that specific time. Comments such as, "She was always a bright young lady" and "I know she is so grateful for the support" were popular conversation starters that resulted in the question, "You heard she is moving down South, right?"

Additionally, as a first-generation, only child of Caribbean parents, my testimony of iniquity was shared internationally with an onslaught of relatives. As an only child birthed by parents' union, I served as one of my mother's few opportunities for "success" as it relates to her parenting abilities and maturation into the "new country." Alternately, even though my father and I spend a substantial amount of time together, our relationship mirrored the product of unresolved childhood trauma. He was thrust into the role of "Father" despite his inconsistent participation in the rearing of his tribe of children. Together they served as my social-emotional foundation and a constant reminder of my glass ceiling limitations.

April 26, 2018

Dear Self,

"I can do all things through Christ which strengtheneth me."

Phillippians 4:13

With over 10 years of experience as an educator, I have never experienced anything like this before. Honestly speaking, up until this point, I was quite comfortable surviving in the normalcy of mundane and repetitious living. Currently, my salary is the same; it was over 7 years ago, and my side hustle consists of tutoring elementary-aged children the fundamentals of reading and writing. Thank the Lord, He saw fit to elevate me and establish me as the Director of Education for this fantastic endeavor.

So here I was, all the way in Anaheim, California preparing to present to a large group of educators. Derived from various regions in our nation, I was charged to help facilitate training about social-emotional learning (SEL). The thrill of being out of the state while school was in session was synonymous to the first time I drove unaccompanied by my driving instructor. On the other hand, the feeling of fear attempted to play an unwarranted game of "peekaboo" and fought vigorously to superimpose his crafty perimeters. Ultimately, my purpose of executing prevailed and quickly gathered the assorted leis to distribute as the guest entered the session.

Finally, the moment had arrived for me to whisper a prayer and stand before the people. My mentor shot a glance in my direction and motioned for me to provide professional input. Surprisingly, I sprang up and mounted the podium like a champ. I was careful to engage the audience, concentrate on my speech inflection, and serve as an emotional polygamist while presenting on the topic of "Emotional Freedom for Educators."

Throughout the room, I witnessed educators sob, cry, and display an array of emotions while seated. One participant eagerly volunteered to share her testimony of feeling anger because of her obligation to raise her young granddaughter. We embraced and applauded her transparency in sharing her story. The session concluded with a mob of attendees waiting patiently to receive strategies to employ in their classrooms and educational spaces.

Today, my faith and self-worth were catapulted to another dimension.

September 28, 2019

Dear Self,

"And the Lord answered me, and said, Write the vision, and make it plain upon tables, that he may run that readeth it.

For the vision is yet for an appointed time, but at the end, it shall speak, and not lie: though it tarry, wait for it; because it will surely come, it will not tarry." Habakkuk 2:2-3

On this day, thirty-seven years ago, a disciple was born. It is my birthday, and the celebration is located at my local library nestled amongst the archives of historical educators while working on my dissertation. Unlike years past, this birthday "turn-up" has been strategically designed to work on the rough draft of my paper and conduct an online meeting with company stakeholders. Since the company has become a global entity, we have been working diligently to work with different institutions to reinstate biblical principles back into the schools.

Since arriving back home, my spiritual growth has ascended tremendously, and the family construct has transformed beyond my one-dimensional mind. My desire to serve within a ministry has been satisfied, and my love for the Kingdom has grown immensely. It is fulfilling to receive fresh manna from heaven and be surrounded by individuals with the obedience to impact a nation. Additionally, not only have the boys settled in, but they are beginning to embrace and operate in their gifts. Their schedules are so strategically ordained; I may have to consider a personal driver. Ugh!

Finally, I am walking in the direction preordained for me from the foundation of the earth. After all, I have been through, who would have ever imagined me in this space? A space filled with promise and the grace to journey onward. Hope. Most importantly, supplemental evidence needed to acquire disciplined discipleship. This is my story of how I learned how to *Get Over It!*

Never let your Disabilities Disable your Abilities or Limit your Possibilities Because The Best is Yet to Come!

~Dr. Adair

Tuesday S. White

Tuesday White is a full-time Editor, and Content Writer who runs her own company,

The W Standard Content & Copy Firm. She's also a lifestyle/self-development blogger and Self-Published Author. Her first book, Soul Repair: *Reshaping, Rebuilding, and Renewing in Pursuit of Self-Mastery,* was published in December 2018. Formerly a Health Insurance Professional, she has a strong background in business protocols and practices, brand management, marketing, and public relations. She's the mother of two daughters, Mona and Ellie, and currently lives in Nassau, The Bahamas.

"When you are who you say are, and you work through all your issues to find the best version of yourself, you will start to see the best in others as well. You will start to see the beauty in the world."

~Tuesday S. White

"Something Good"

In my own personal pursuit of self-mastery, I have been teaching myself that everything can be used for something good. I've learned that most things that seemed hard only become harder when they're not addressed when and how they should be.

I have learned to face adversity with the end goal of finding an alleviating solution that will either repair the situation or eradicate it altogether.

I have learned to be kinder with myself, gentler with others, yet firm with my convictions.

Yes, this pursuit is molding me in a way where everything CAN ABSOLUTELY be something good. Every experience is an opportunity to learn and grow.

As a full-time content writer and copy editor, I am privileged to read some of the amazing stories from people of all walks of life. These memoirs, reflections, and testimonies truly touch me, as I told one publisher the other day.

In the beginning, my perspective was much different.

I would get annoyed by long narratives that were poorly written and thus not very clear. It seemed tedious to go through thousands of words and hundreds of pages where subject and verb were in disagreement, punctuation sometimes non-existent, and correct spelling seemed somewhat optional. I viewed a lot of the work that came across my computer as a burden, forgetting that I had chosen this as a part of my calling.

Midway through the various books, articles, and essays, there was a plot twist of sorts in the way my mind received what it was taking in.

As I was working on myself, I opened up in a way that I can only describe as a beautiful blossoming.

Everything was about to become something good.

Now, as I edit and reformat these books, there is no annoyance, there is no irritation. All that is there is purpose and productivity.

These people had amazing stories to tell, and useful knowledge to impart. They are brilliant in their own respects. They are taking an integral step in their careers and lives by sharing their stories or work with the world.

They are taking a step that even I, as a writer, has been afraid to take. They are in the process of becoming published.

And, they have chosen me to edit their work. They have given me the job of ensuring that the words that are their stories, and that define their work are the right words. They are writing books and publishing them the right way; by getting a good publisher who ensures that they get a good editor.

I'm the good editor who was chosen. I have been granted access to the stories behind the mastery they have achieved in some aspects of their lives.

I've been touched by the humility of some of these clients as they graciously accept my editing and restructuring of their work. It is respected on a professional level. They put confidence in what I do, and they even sometimes send more business my way.

So, tell me, what form of a wretch would I be if I stayed up on that high horse, judging them for not being as skilled as I am at doing what I do for a living?

These are people who would run circles around me in their fields if I were ever to give it a try. They're beating me at my own race by becoming published before me, and I'm an actual full-time writer.

They have come to me for what I do best, and for that, I am thankful.

I have gone from being known as a harsh grammar critic to a purposeful editor who seeks to ensure that each published author that crosses my path puts his/her best foot forward. I am here to get the writing right.

This lesson professionally and personally has been a huge one. It's been one that I should have applied to my life over a decade ago.

It has shown me, in this season and moment of my life, how I let one of the things that seemed hard, get even harder over time. I'm able to see now how I made bad situations worse, and how the difference in my approach was a miscued, misguided perspective.

My Decade of Deviance 2007-2017

In those ten years, as I reflect, I realize that I did just about everything possible to stand in my own way.

I put up a defense against the tough love of family and true friends. I ran away from my issues, and over time, hid them so far back that it appeared as though they didn't exist.

I was a walking conundrum. At times even, an empty barrel making a lot of noise.

I was reckless, careless, and thoughtless at some intervals.

In 2007, I was 28 years old, between jobs and highly dysfunctional relationships.

It has occurred to me, upon reflection, that not only did I have horrible taste in men, I also have a penchant for bringing out the worst in them.

I was a glamour girl in those days and was all about my labels and my social life. In truth, I was a bit out of control, partying way too much up until about 2013.

I was all over the place. I went from club to pub to bar to a house party, to parking lot concerts, and backyard "bashments." My friends and I were on every guest list, in all the right skyboxes, on the best trips, controlling the social scene one night at a time.

Fortunately for me, my 8-year-old daughter's father was very active in her life, so she was shielded from a lot of my antics and poor associations.

I loved the limelight. I had worked in the amazing Atelier of a renowned local fashion designer with a high-profile international clientele. My day to day job allowed me to play around with design and décor. I attended high society events regularly and was featured in the newspapers rubbing shoulders with the Who's Who.

It seemed likely that the lifestyle I was living was one I would retain to appease my materialism. However, what the public saw drastically differed from my life behind closed doors.

None of my relationships ended well. By this time, I had already been physically abused by two men.

I had a temper that made me forget myself often. And, while no man should feel at liberty to hit a woman, I often propelled arguments to violence and other destructive behavior.

Yes, for all my vanity and self-centeredness, I had been hit in the face and bruised about the body, and, still, I stayed. I stayed because I felt that jealousy was an obvious sign of deep love from these men.

I stayed because I was a blessing blocking, narrow-minded bigot.

No one could tell me anything about me, constructively. I would choose the beautiful lies and deception of men who were only using me over the logical, yet hard to hear truth that could set me on the right course.

It had to end, and so, after a series of dramatic events, one night, it did.

On a Friday evening, an argument with my boyfriend at the time took an ugly turn. He was drunk and belligerently accusing me of cheating on him. My insolence and refusal to back down from his verbal threats were not received well.

He eventually snatched my phone and car keys and told me,

"The only way you're leaving here is in a body bag."

At that moment, I remember my stomach flipped over, and my heart began beating faster than ever before. I had to find a way out of that house because there was no way I was going to end up dead at the hands of this coward.

So, I acted swiftly. When he staggered off to use the bathroom in his stupor, I fled through the bedroom sliding door, barefooted, out the front gate, and into the street.

That was the first time I had ever been able to get that sliding door open. It had a faulty latch that required a man's strength to release. But, this was not a night for feminine frailty. I bruised and almost broke my fingers getting that door open.

Once out of the yard, I remember the street lights looking hazy if I were in a dream. I thought quickly as I darted across the road and ran a very short distance to a neighbor's house seeking refuge.

She let me in startled but without question. She could see something was wrong, and the fear in my face was enough to tell her that I needed safety at that very moment.

I had to call the police that night, go back to the house with them, and collect my car and some belongings.

It was an awful experience. It was one of my lowest moments. Yet, at the very same time, it was one of my bravest acts.

I vividly recall the lights blurring as I ran by them that night, barefoot, in tears, with no money, phone, or real plan. At the same time, great pressure was lifted from me as the night air-dried my tears.

I felt free. I was saving myself. I was brave.

If only I could have duplicated that bravery in years to come.

That girl, who had had enough, was willing to leave empty-handed that night. I was willing to save my own life because I knew there would be something better for me.

I wish in the years that followed that I would have seen more of that girl.

But I had a long, long way to go. The body of work that God had placed within me wouldn't and couldn't surface in that decade.

It would be a few years before I would end up at the proverbial crosswords of "Do" or "Die."

That relationship inevitably ended amid bitter discourse and continuing disagreement over the division of assets and property. I ended up abandoning the home that I owned and was still financially responsible.

I would rather seek peace and resolve of my own state of mind at my father's house than to be in an environment riddled with bad memories.

Eventually, I moved into a new place. Soon after, I was able to get a job with a prestigious corporate firm.

It was now 2008, and this would be a "good part" for a few years in some ways. I excelled professionally, learning so much in my tenure with this company. I was able to make great connections with businesspersons, and the networking opportunities were excellent.

The learning and training were sometimes intense, and I felt my superiors were hard on me. But, the lessons have been priceless and the backbone and structure of my own business today.

While I did well career-wise, I still carried around a lot of anger, insecurity, and darkness from my previous tumultuous relationships. When I started dating again in late 2009, it came as an opportunity to be happy. We were friends; my family loved this guy. We were inseparable.

Somehow, I let the old fears destroy what we were building. While I was caring and attentive, I was also needy regarding attention. I was significantly affected by others around me and would wage war against anyone who seemed to try and bring trouble into my camp.

Yes, I was hot-headed and would rise to any occasion to stir something up. It was juvenile and unbecoming. My behavior didn't match my profile. I was supposed to be an executive and somewhat of a literary genius. But, I could be found in common arguments if someone didn't look at me right.

I think that in late 2011 when that relationship ended, I essentially broke my own heart. I was my own undoing. In a brief conversation in my driveway just days before Christmas that year, he told me,

"I just can't do it anymore."

The few days after were hard. I was pissed off. Then, I was sad. And, then, I let him go. Despite being upset, feeling abandoned and misunderstood, I let him go. I knew deep down that I could not, in my mental state, give him what he needed.

Around that same time, my tenure with my beloved corporate job came to an end. To be honest, I quit on a whim where I felt I was ready to branch out on my own.

In truth, at that time, I was underqualified to even say the word, "Entrepreneur." I was unprepared and unstable. It ended before it started.

I went back into the job market the following year. Around that same time, my father's health started to decline. My sister and I moved into a family home in East Nassau where he could have his own space, and we could feel comforted knowing that we were near when he needed us. He was known in those days to dismiss housekeepers or nurses we tried to have around to keep an eye on him.

After that last relationship, I dated casually, but I didn't have the heart or interest to take anything or anyone serious.

My daughter was becoming a teenager now, she needed me even more. So, I shifted my focus.

Still, as I was struggling to align myself again, to restore the grandeur of years past, I was failing. I wasn't adding up. I felt I was falling short.

My only recourse was that this little girl never loved me less. She would brighten up my days even when I was insisting on wallowing in self-pity and depression.

In late November 2013, an emergency room visit for my father would end up being the last time he would see the world outside of Doctors Hospital in Nassau, The Bahamas.

He went in with a stomach ache that led to further tests that confirmed he needed surgery and ended up in the ICU fighting for his life.

By the time the surgery was done, the doctors had explained that his body, frail from months of illness, was failing him.

On Nov 26th, 2013, at 11:46pm, he died. It was a Tuesday.

My family and I buried him on Sunday, December 8th, 2013, honoring him within an elaborate High Mass funeral at his beloved St. Agnes Anglican Church, in Grant's Town, Nassau.

I remember each detail because I was there through every single moment of it. From the time he got sick, to the time of death, to the time they came for his body. Then, there was the business of planning a funeral, picking his clothes, the order of service, the scripture readings, the casket, the headstone, and the church band's rendition of "Abide with me" I chose for when they lowered him into his grave.

It all changed me. I made me look at life as a whole differently.

In the months to follow, I made my second attempt at entrepreneurship by way of a public relations and events firm. That was January 2014, and by October of that year, it was a bust.

It seemed my heart was in the right place, but my focus wasn't there. I couldn't seem to make it stick. I didn't believe that it would stick. And so, it didn't.

Later that year, on a desperate hunt, I found another job in the corporate Bahamas in the same industry as the first one that I had loved so much.

I went into 2015 on a high. I was ready to feel accomplished again. I was eager to be a part of an innovative team.

It did happen briefly.

I was given a platform where I could define my job within specific parameters. I was able to provide this greener company the best of what I took concerning skills and abilities from the seasoned firm who was their competitor.

It was great, in the beginning.

And still, something was happening with me that seemed to be contradicting my current life.

I was productive, building up a career, yet what I was building seemed to be the perfect platform for someone else.

I was really good at what I was doing. I was using my knowledge in a certain field to support this new company's new and growing portfolio. I was a part of a team effort at innovation.

But, what I was writing and reading all day was far-fetched from the kind of content I wanted to create for myself. I couldn't clearly define or outline my own branding and direction. I was swamped with the demands of the job.

There was no time for me to produce at a good level and invest time in my personal ideas.

There was no time, it seemed.

I started to get uncomfortable. As I was, I was doing well, but there was really nowhere for me to grow outside the box that I was placed in.

I knew it was time to go when I started shifting the blame on the company, my managers, and even the whole employment system for me feeling as "stuck" as I was.

I had misplaced entirely the fact that I had applied for and taken the position with no gun to my head or mandate from governing powers.

As I became more and more uncomfortable, I started teetering on insubordination on the job toward my superiors.

I was determined to move forward with my own ideas, develop my brand, and make it work this time. I had remodeled my business plan away from providing physical services to online sales, affiliate marketing, and content management.

In mid-2016, I resigned from my job. This time, I had a plan that was seemingly foolproof and only needed the time, dedication, and skill to flourish.

I was ready.

In the first few months, I was able to earn enough money in one month to cover my expenses for the next quarter. I had found a way to maximize online advertisements and the power of SEO on content and affiliate links.

All seemed well at first. It was cutting edge the way I was able to join other bloggers and affiliate marketers at reaping the rewards of long hours of content creation and management.

But for me, this couldn't be it.

I was writing my own content now, but it wasn't really representative of what I really wanted to say. Instead, I was feeding into the appeal of trending topics that were popular and sought after across websites and social media. I was moving further and further away from the truth, hiding behind popular opinion and likable content.

In the months that followed, I wasn't able to keep up with the demands of the internet. My monthly income started to dwindle, and I was losing direction more and more every day.

Something had to give. And it did.

I found myself pregnant with my second child. By January 2017, the whole structure of my life was about to shift again, and uncertainty was at every angle I looked.

I decided this could be the time to move away from my current environment, gather my thoughts, and refresh.

I was right and wrong at the same time.

There was some turbulence I would have to endure before I could get to the good part.

I had a healthy pregnancy and gave birth to a beautiful baby girl in July of 2017. It was a wonderful moment, bringing her into the world.

But, in the 9 months, before she came, I experienced some of the worst times of my life.

No one was physically abusing me, but there were many who victimized me for my choice of having my daughter. Despite not knowing the details of the circumstances, I became the underdog, the scapegoat in a bad situation, and the brunt of many bad jokes and tasteless rumors.

Even now, as I reflect, there is no way that I can find justifiable cause for the way things happened then. Despite the misdirection of my moral compass, I really didn't do anything so terrible that was worthy of the sensationalism and speculation it garnered.

It got to a point where I had to stop myself from responding to the rumors and inaccuracies. I had to allow many to show their true colors without rendering retribution to them for their deeds.

I got through the months that followed merely eking by. I had spent a good part of a year distracted by the ramifications of heartless gossip, and the dynamics of the unconventional situation with my infant daughter and all those involved.

This was around the time that I finally started to see a clear outline for my business. I could see now what I was supposed to be doing, I just needed to find a way to get things going.

In my research, when trying to align my thoughts with these aspirations, I started reading more and more about mindfulness and self-mastery.

It made me take an honest look at myself one day in January 2018.

I was an emotional mess that day, I could hardly breathe. My heart was hurting in a way I had never experienced. I started praying for answers and talking aloud to myself in my empty apartment.

I had a plan, but I did not know how to execute it. I did not have the confidence to start. I could almost reach out and touch my future success, but I didn't know how to move all of the things that were blocking me.

I remembered a saying then that I always brought to mind whenever a loved one was lost,

"Pain is the breaking of the shell that contains our understanding."

It was from the teachings of The Prophet Khalil Gibran.

Although I had used it often, this was most certainly the time that it held real significance to me.

On that emotional day, I was breaking into pieces; my heart, mind, and soul were opening, and what was coming in all at once was the raw and real honesty about where I was, what was happening, and who I was to become.

I started packing everything up. I was throwing out the things I didn't need and organizing what I would take with me.

I called my mother in tears of heartache and enlightenment and told her that I needed to come home and have her help me get my life in order.

As I was packing, I started mentally offloading all the hurt and disappointments from my past and present.

I started forgiving myself and everyone for all the wrong. I started thanking God for every blessing I could now see clearly.

I had a wonderful family, I had good health, I had financial support, and the capability to build a business and sustain it.

Just about everything I needed was within my reach, and what wasn't, I was well on my way to achieving.

I started slowly building up my business. I watched it over the next few months take its form. I lined up my skills, and for each one, I created a product that I could offer to my clients. I then got back to blogging.

This time, I removed the advertisements, I stopped coordinating SEO and keywords, and I let myself write the truth.

It was ugly, and then it was beautiful. I was glowing through a period of growth.

The more I wrote from my heart, sharing my struggles and triumphs, the more the readers came. The more I opened up about my journey of trying to cover so much ground in a short period, the closer I got to my goal.

I was happily going through the hard parts, thankful for my abilities and evolving perspective.

By September of this year, I started writing my first book. It is a narrative in detail of my life and the lesson I've learned along the way. It's a story of evolution.

Somehow, once I got past the outline, I started to lose my way. This is when I turned to my journal and notes and started piecing together an outline to motivate myself to keep going and finish the book.

What happened then was phenomenal. I ended up writing a book that would help me to write the book I had already started.

Soul Repair – Reshaping, Rebuilding, and Renewing in Pursuit of Self-Mastery has taken its place among the self-help books of the world, and I have no words to define how proud I am.

I fought through it and gave my notes, methods, thoughts, and motivation to the world.

I finally joined the ranks of those amazing, empowering people I edit for. I have finally become a woman I can depend on to keep making *me* proud.

All of the years spent chasing the wrong things became the stories behind the lessons. I started standing firmly and unashamed in my truth, owning all of the difficulties of my past and, in turn, owning every single moment that I triumphed over it.

I came full circle. I have come a long from the girl who ran barefoot in the street to save her life.

She was brave at that moment, but still had a long way to go.

I made that journey for her.

Today, I remember her, and I am brave over and over again, despite any obstacles I may encounter.

I am humbled by the blessing of good friends and family in my life who never let me scrape the bottom. I am thankful for a mother who prays and understands.

I am thankful for me. I broke many self-inflicted curses to revive the goodness in me and to prepare myself for what comes next.

I speak candidly of my "Fortified Future" with a smile and obvious anticipation. I will be 40 in 2019, and I've themed the beginning of a new decade as "Forty-Fied." It's very fitting. It's like diving alignment.

It is something good to look forward to.

I would not be here today to write this if I hadn't committed to changing my perspective to change my life.

If I have any advice for you, it is simple.

Don't let anyone hit you.

Carry yourself like a Queen from this moment forward. Think of yourself like a Queen and a person of value. Put your best foot forward, and I guarantee you that the people who matter will take note.

When you are who you say are, and you work through all your issues to find the best version of yourself, you will start to see the best in others as well. You will begin to see the beauty in the world.

That's how I edit these days. I see the beauty in the story or body of work, and I do my part to let that shine through.

And, that is a good thing.

Some dreams do come with an expiration date. Especially if you don't do the work to fulfill them.

~Dr. Adair

When you are drowning in
Fear, Confusion, and
Doubt, remember your
Faith can always save
you.

~Dr. Adair

The best part of hitting rock bottom
is knowing that there's no place else to go
but UP.

~Dr. Adair

The hardest part about
Forgiveness is when you
have to do it again, and
again, and again.

~Dr. Adair

*Based on Matthew 18:22

"To Thine Own Self Be True…"

~William Shakespeare

Concluding Thoughts
Dr. Adair

So there you have it.

10 authors. 10 stories.

And, 10 different stories to help you learn how to **Get Over It!**

It definitely is a journey, but the route belongs to you.

Know it. Claim it.

Stand in your truth.

Live in your purpose.

Persevere in your passion.

Know that when you are not moving, you're flying because the clouds belong to you.

The universe is abundant with joy and happiness.

Give yourself permission to grab a piece of it.

I know you can do it.

I know you have to do it.

Because it's the best way to **Get Over It!**

About the Publisher

Dr. Adair is the international multiple bestselling author of *Go Hard and Stumble Softly* published in July 2012 and *Get Over It! 7 Steps to Live Well with Lupus*. She is also the author of *Get Over It! How to Bounce Back After Hitting Rock Bottom, How to Get Over It! in 30 Days Parts I, II, and III Get Over It! How to Bounce Back After Hitting Rock Bottom for Teens and White Girl Speaks Powerful Words of Inspiration for Leadership and Success in Your Life!* Her 2017 releases include *21 Ways to Get Over It! And 21 Ways to Get Over It for Teens* and the accompanying journals. Her first anthology, *"Get Over It!: Stories of Release, Resilience, Redemption, and Resurrection,"* was published in March 2018.

In addition to the titles above, Dr. Adair has published multiple books for other authors via her publishing company, Johnson Tribe Publishing, and has helped propel their titles to Bestseller status. She created an award-winning leadership and personal development curriculum and program for teens and her latest curriculum that focuses on Teen Dating Violence.

In addition to writing and publishing, Dr. Adair is a popular and dynamic international speaker with expertise in various topics. She has also been featured in *The Huffington Post, Black Enterprise, Rolling Out, POSE, Glambitious, BOLD* magazines, and on *CBS 46 Atlanta television*. Dr. Adair has appeared on several *national* and *international* radio shows, podcasts and is the recipient of several academic and civic awards.

Dr. Adair earned her Ph.D. from the University at Buffalo and received a master's degree in the counseling field. She is married and the mother of five children.

Other Books by Dr. Adair

9 781733 784412